THE TWO ROADS TO DIVORCE

THE TWO ROADS TO DIVORCE

Lenard Marlow

Library of Congress Number: 2003095179
ISBN: Hardcover 1-4134-2282-9
Softcover 1-4134-2281-0

This book was printed in the United States of America.

To order additional copies of this book, contact:
Xlibris Corporation
1-888-795-4274
www.Xlibris.com
Orders@Xlibris.com
20417

CONTENTS

PART III
Finding Your Way—Avoiding the Hazards

PART IV
The Fork in the Road

To Max Cohen, a good friend, colleague and teacher

To my wife, Marilyn, with whom I have been arguing successfully now for more than thirty-five years

I wish to express my thanks to my good friend and colleague, Barbara Badolato, for her invaluable contributions to this book.

There is no human enterprise entered into
with as much expectation, fraught with as much
disappointment, as marriage.

PREFACE

When someone asks me what I do, I say that I am a divorce lawyer by profession of origin but a divorce mediator by profession of choice. Those are the two roads I have traveled down in my professional life.

They are very different roads. In fact, they are very different worlds of understanding in terms of what divorce represents. When divorcing husbands and wives go down one of those roads, they are viewed as having a legal problem. Admittedly, it has certain personal implications. Nevertheless, it is seen as being primarily a legal problem, which is why lawyers are the ones principally involved.

When the two of them go down the other road, they are viewed as having a personal problem. To be sure, their divorce has certain legal implications. But it is basically a personal problem. That is why, though lawyers are involved, it is the parties themselves who will make all the important decisions.

In large measure, this book represents what I have witnessed and learned in my travels down these two different roads. I wrote it, in part, because I wanted husbands and wives faced with their own divorce to have the benefit of my experience before they decided which of those roads they would take themselves.

I also wrote it for another reason. For almost forty years now, my professional life has been devoted to helping husbands and wives address the practical problems they suddenly found themselves faced with as a result of their decision to divorce. In that time, I have read many of the books dealing with divorce that they themselves turned to for help. I have long felt that they were ill served by most of them. In fact, I came to the conclusion that those books invariably sent them off in the wrong direction.

I felt they deserved better. Divorce is difficult enough as it is. Those going through it do not need to be left more overwhelmed and frightened than they already are.

I wrote this book for one last reason. I wanted to offer hope to those going through this very difficult period in their lives. It would be irresponsible for me to paint pretty pictures for you, or to tell you that you do not have anything to worry about. Nevertheless, I do want to convince you that as dark as things may now appear, if you will think and act carefully, rather than just react emotionally, there can be light at the end of the road. Not as a certainty. Nothing in life is certain. Nevertheless, as a real possibility. I will not tell you that you will be able to see that light tomorrow. In the real world that we live in, things take time. You will therefore have to be patient. But with time and effort, it can happen.

I appreciate that it will be difficult if not impossible for you to see this now. That is why you will need the eyes of someone who is able to see it for you. That is why you will need someone to inspire you to hope, and to give you reason to have hope. I would very much like to do that. However, I will first have to point you in the right direction. Otherwise, like so many divorcing husbands and wives before you, you will only go off in the wrong direction and end up getting lost.

PART I

Starting Out

CHAPTER 1

DISPOSABLE MARRIAGES

People do not get divorced because they want to get divorced.
They get divorced because they don't know what else to do.

We often hear it said that we live in a disposable society. If something doesn't work, or we tire of it, we simply throw it away. After all, we can always get a new and better one.

That supposedly applies to marriage as well. Thus, it is often suggested that when someone gets tired or bored with their husband or wife, or if problems arise in their marriage, they simply dispose of them. They get a divorce. It is as easy as changing a pair of shoes.

Nothing could be further from the truth. It may be true of television sets and automobiles, but it isn't true of marriage. In fact, contrary to what you may hear or think, people do not make the decision to divorce too quickly. If anything, they wait too long.

If you are the one who is seriously considering a separation or divorce, or has already made that decision, you don't need to be told this. You know it from your own experience. In all likelihood, you have been contemplating this decision for a year or more. You have been unhappy, in many cases desperately unhappy, for much longer than that. Looking back, you may even feel that you have been unhappy from the day you got married. Or, as with many people, there may have been a period of time, even a long period, when the marriage was basically a satisfying one. However, that was a long time ago. You did not make the decision to divorce the first time something went wrong. You didn't even do that the tenth or eleventh time. Rather, there have been so many things, and you have been desperately unhappy for so long, that you have lost count.

Nor did you want to divorce. It was the last thing that you wanted, and you did everything you could to avoid it. For years, you have walked around and around your marriage hoping to find some place that would give, some way to improve it. You did not like the very hard choice you were given, which was either to stay in a marriage that denied to you what you felt were your most essential needs or to throw over the entire structure of your life—and, if you have children, theirs as well. The last thing that you wanted was to be where you are today. But there was nothing that you could do to prevent it. No matter what you said or what you did, your husband or wife simply would not change. As far as you could tell, they did not even hear you. Nor, after a point, were you able to live with the way things were. You were literally drowning and suffocating in your marriage and it was having a terrible effect on you, emotionally and even physically.

That is why all of this talk about disposable marriages is so inappropriate and even irresponsible. It makes light of something that could not be more serious. People do not get divorced because they want to get divorced. They get divorced because they don't know what else to do.

So much for the idea that the problem with marriage today is that we have developed a cavalier attitude toward divorce, or that we have made divorce too easy. So much for the simplistic belief that all we need is a moral shot in the arm—a renewed commitment to moral values—and all will be well. You know better than that.

It wasn't for not caring. It wasn't for lack of trying. It was because nothing would change. It was because you could no longer live with it the way it was. And it was because it was only getting worse.

CHAPTER 2

THE GARDEN OF EDEN

Husbands and wives commonly divorce one another for the very reasons that they married one another.

When something goes wrong, it is natural to look for an explanation. After all, everything must have a cause. The same is true of divorce. There must be a reason. Or, as the law has traditionally put it, someone must be at "fault."

This belief derives from our view of the world, which is grounded in the story of the Garden of Eden. That story tells us that the disharmony that we see everywhere between man and nature is not an inherent part of the human condition or, therefore, inevitable. Rather, what caused Adam and Eve to be expelled from the Garden of Eden (to fall from grace) was human failing (sin). However, that harmony could be restored if human conduct could be purged of its transgressions. Then, as we are taught, the lion will lie down with the lamb, and men will beat their swords into plowshares and not make war with one another any more.

Our view of marriage and divorce is grounded in the same understanding. Like Adam and Eve, who originally lived in a perfect state of harmony with the world in the Garden of Eden, we believe that husbands and wives did as well. Accordingly, the disharmony that led to their divorce was not an inherent part of their marriage. It was not there "in the beginning." Rather, their falling out of love (the "fall from grace") was caused by the misconduct of one of them. That is what we mean when we say that the divorce was caused by one of the parties—that it was his or her "fault." If one of them had not been guilty of misconduct, they would still have a happy marriage (still be in love). Put simply, marriages do not have to end in divorce. Rather, like the endings of the fairy tales that were read to us as children, we believe that it is possible for husbands and wives to live "happily ever after." Moreover, the harmony in their marriage could still be restored and their marriage saved if the guilty party would only mend his or her ways.

This view of marriage and divorce is deeply embedded in our thinking. It is why our legal system has traditionally viewed divorce as a grade-B western made up of good guys and bad guys. It is also why actions for divorce have had the air of quasi-criminal proceedings. Moreover, despite our more liberal divorce laws—which more reflect society's desire to permit divorce than they do any real change in our understanding of it—this view still informs much of our thinking.

It is understandable that husbands and wives who are locked in an unhappy marriage will view it this way—see themselves as being unhappy because of what the other has done or been unwilling to do. They are too close to what has happened to see it clearly and too emotionally involved in it to look at it objectively. As a result, they feel too much and understand too little. But why do the rest of us, who are able to view their marriage more dispassionately and from more of a distance, not see it any more clearly?

There are a number of reasons for this. The first, as I said, derives from our Garden of Eden cosmology. Since we see their marriage as having been initially perfect, it cannot have been anything that was inherent in their relationship. After all, everyone who attended their wedding will testify that they were completely in love then, and that nothing was out of place. If that is so, it must be something that happened (was introduced into their relationship) later.

The second reason may surprise you. It is that we really do not know why husbands and wives get divorced. Put another way, we do not know any more about why they stop being in love than we do about why they fell in love in the first place. We do not have a clue. And so, even though the two of them are the least reliable witnesses when it comes to their own marriage, we will invariably accept everything they tell us at face value. If they say that their husband or wife was at "fault", and particularly if they give us chapter and verse to support it, we will accept it as gospel. But, then, not having any better explanation, what else can we do?

Unfortunately, being biased observers, the report we will be given will leave out many of the essential ingredients. Put another way, it will tell us what happened, but not why. As a result, it will cause us to make the most common mistake when it comes to divorce. That is to confuse the symptom of the problem (the disharmony in their marriage) for its cause. That is to look at the things husbands and wives do and say and the way in which they act when they are unhappy in their marriage, and see that as the cause of the problem rather than its symptom. It is to look at the wrong starting point.

Why are husbands and wives such biased observers? Because, when someone is unhappy in their marriage, it will never occur to them that they could have had anything to do with the problem (their unhappiness). Rather, they will invariably attribute it to their husband or wife. They are unhappy because of what their husband or wife has done or been unwilling to do. That is the problem, and if their husband or wife would only act differently (change), there wouldn't be any problem. Thus, when they tell the history of their marriage, and when it began to have problems, that will be their starting point—the point when they began to be unhappy.

That is not how their husband or wife will tell the history of their marriage, however. To begin with, in most instances, they will not see themselves as having done anything wrong, or at least anything so terribly wrong. They will certainly not see it as the great crime that their husband or wife makes it out to be. Even if they do acknowledge that they had something to do with the problem, as on occasion they must, since they will not suffer the same pain on its account, it will not have the significance for them that it does for their husband or wife. As a result, they will feel that their husband or wife is making too much of it, and that they should get past it, let go of it, and go on. In fact, from their standpoint, it will be their husband's or wife's unwillingness to do this, and their constant harping on old grievances, that will constitute the problem in the marriage. Thus, when they tell the history of their marriage and its problems, not seeing their own role in any of this, or minimizing it even if they do, they will have a very different starting point. It will be their husband's or wife's inappropriate conduct, not their own. I often express this to couples who come to me for help by saying: "While the two of you may have been married to one another, you come to me with very different histories of your marriage. If I could get you to agree on the history of your marriage, I could probably save your marriage. But I am not going to be able to do that."

That is why all of their discussions (their attempts to address the problems in their marriage) will be so unproductive and so painful. That is also why neither of them will feel that the other has understood a word they have said. Having such different starting points, and organizing their experience so differently, all that they will do is "talk past one another" rather than "with one another."

Not uncommonly, husbands and wives will explain this by saying that their problem is one of a "lack of communication." That is not their problem. Their problem is that, since they come to their discussions with such different histories of their marriage, and since so much hurt and anger has built up between them over this, they no longer have anything to say to one another. How could they when they do not have a common history? It is for this same reason that someone who has listened to each of them describe the history of their marriage will come away feeling that they have heard stories about different marriages, not the same one.

Unfortunately, their telling of the story will do more than cause them to confuse the symptom of the problem for its cause. It will also change its characterization. Their failed expectations, their consequent hurt and disappointment, and the misunderstanding it has engendered, represent a terrible tragedy in their lives. However, seeing it through the lens of their hurt and disappointment, the story they will tell us will not be about a tragedy. It will be about a crime.

CHAPTER 3

WHOSE FAULT IS IT?

Husbands and wives do not get divorced because they are good people or bad people. They get divorced because they are different people.

Whenever I am asked why husbands and wives divorce, usually reply, "Because they are desperately unhappy," and leave it at that. Since, at least initially, most divorces are initiated by one person rather than two, it would be more accurate for me to say that it is because one of them is desperately unhappy.

Though the answer I have given is the correct one, it is not the one that those who asked the question expected. They were looking for something more. They wanted to know what took place in the marriage that led to the divorce. If I give them the answer I do, it is because I want to frustrate their tendency to look for simple answers to explain complex problems. It is because I do not want to reinforce their tendency to see the symptom of the problem (the conduct of one of them) as its cause.

Why do we all make this mistake? Again, it derives from our Garden of Eden view of marriage. We see the couple as having started out in a perfect state of harmony—as being at one with one another. We get so taken in by the fact that they were in love we fail to see that there was always a divisive element in their relationship. We get so taken in by the harmony in the Garden of Eden that we fail to see the serpent.

What is it that our Garden of Eden view of marriage prevents us from seeing? It is that, in a very important sense, all marriages are mismatches. They are made up of two very different people. Worse, brides and grooms are not generally aware of those differences, which accounts for the saying that we marry half-strangers. On some level at least, couples may be aware that those differences exist. Nevertheless, the very strong feelings they are experiencing, as well as other factors, will tend to mute this. They may even give the illusion that there are none, and that the two of them are completely "as one." But, like love itself, that is only an illusion.

Ironically, it is not uncommon that people can now tell you things that took place prior to their marriage, that were tell-tale signs of the problems to come, that they did not see then. (They could not tell you about them now if they did not see them then. They just didn't want to look at them.) There are others who will tell you that they realized they had made a mistake literally the day they got married, or very shortly thereafter.

This is a testament to the power of the feelings that overwhelm our critical faculties. They enable us to hold up pretty pictures for ourselves. They cause us to be taken in by the fairy tale endings portrayed to us on the covers of literally all our magazines—of Prince Charming awakening Sleeping Beauty. Worse, they disable us from being able to see any of the things that would call them into question.

The problem is that we do not see those feelings as representing a hindrance, let alone a disability. In part, that is because we have been brought up to see the feelings we are experiencing as representing the expression of our noblest aspirations, and what is best in us. But it is also because those feelings fulfill such important needs of ours that they overpower us. They literally carry us away. Unfortunately, having been brought up on fairy tales, no one warns us that they are a potion that will put our critical faculties to sleep.

Even if one of the parties does recognize the potential problems, as they sometimes do, more often than not they will tend to discount them. They will buy into their faith that "love will conquer all" and not give them the attention they deserve.

Nevertheless, those differences are there, and they will surface later, when those strong feelings and other factors tend to lose some of their force, as they inevitably will. It is then, when they find themselves confronted with the sheer "otherness of the other," that reality will set in.

The differences that I am talking about are not differences in interests—that one of them likes to play golf and the other tennis. While their relationship will obviously be more satisfying if they have common interests, most couples are able to accommodate these differences, even when they are fairly extreme. For example, I have never seen a couple who divorced because of differences they had over politics or even religion. Rather, what I am referring to are their different personal characteristics and, even more important, their different adaptive styles—their different ways of organizing their lives and doing business. In fact, one might say that their marriage is their ongoing act of negotiating and accommodating those stylistic differences.

Unfortunately, when those different styles clash, as they so often do, they will lead to serious problems. If the two of them are not able to work out an accommodation between those differences, they will eventually lead to their divorce. That is because they will not see them as simply differences in style. Since they will each take for granted their own style and not see anything unusual or inappropriate in it, the other's style, which runs such interference with their own, will appear as the problem. Worse, it will appear as a grievous crime. That is because it will make living with the other person difficult if not impossible. Why is that? Because the party who is unhappy in the marriage will not want to change his or her own adaptive style. Nor will they be able to change the other's style or the effect that it is having on them. Not being able to get around it, they will continually run into it. That will be their problem. As I said, it will eventually lead to their divorce.

To be sure, there are exceptions to this—situations in which the problem in the marriage cannot be explained just in terms of differences in style. For example, there are situations in which one of the parties goes through a sudden, dramatic life change. There are also instances where someone has been guilty of serious misconduct, such as substance abuse or spousal abuse. Even here, however, the relationship between that misconduct and the ultimate divorce is not a simple one, as is witnessed by the fact that rarely does the misconduct lead to an immediate divorce. Rather, the marriage will usually persevere for years, and sometimes forever, despite the misconduct.

There is another exception, as well. Every marriage has a San Andreas fault line running though it—a weak point that will give if too much pressure is applied to it. Generally, husbands and wives are able to dance around that fault line and thereby avoid it. However, certain things can occur which will make that more difficult, if not impossible. That is the case if there has been a very sudden change in their lives, a serious reversal in their fortunes or, worse, a tragedy in their lives, such as the death of a child. Very few marriages survive the death of a child. A tragedy of this magnitude will expose the fault line, put too much pressure on it, and it will give.

Nevertheless, these are the exception not the rule. In most instances, the friction is caused by the ordinary, not the extraordinary. The proof of this is the fact that it is not uncommon for husbands and wives to divorce one another for the very reasons they married one another. What was once the glue that held the relationship together is now the acid that is eating it away. When I mention this to couples who have been married for a relatively short period of time, I commonly get a smile of recognition from one of them—usually the one initiating the divorce. If I do not get the same smile from those who have been married for a longer period of time, it is not because it is any less true. It is just that so much has happened, and so much hurt has built up over the years of their marriage, that they are no longer able to see this.

Let me give you an example of this. In the early years of my practice, when I was still a divorce lawyer, a woman who had married when she was very young consulted me. She had literally gone from her father's home to her husband's home. "What attracted you to your husband when you first met him?" I asked her. "He knew where he was going. He was able to take charge. He got things done," she replied. It was not difficult to understand how someone who had always been dependent on someone else could have been attracted to those traits. But that was seventeen years ago. Things were different now. She was older. Her view of herself had changed. She was also less dependent. "What is the problem now?" I asked again. "It always has to be his way. He never takes into consideration how I feel. He is a bully." She was divorcing him for the very reason that she had married him.

We do not see this because we do not want to see it. If we saw it, we would have to ask questions that we do not want to ask. We might even have to question our decision to marry, and we don't want to do that either. In fact, that is the principal function of the feelings we allow to so overwhelm us. They enable us to avoid asking difficult questions. Better yet, they answer them even when we do raise them. Love, after all, is the argument that admits of no argumentation. To be sure, there are times when those questions surface and the relationship is terminated or the proposed marriage called off. More often than not, however, we brush them under the carpet and do not see them until we have no choice.

There is something else that contributes to the problem. That is how husbands and wives act when those stylistic differences begin to surface and they become unhappy in their marriages. It is also how they will each view the other's actions and, in turn, what their reaction will be. That is what I referred to earlier as the mistake of confusing the symptom of the problem with its cause. Unfortunately, this will only add further weight to what is already an overburdened relationship. Not being able to see their own role in any of this—how their conduct contributed to what has happened—their husband's or wife's inappropriate conduct will seem to be without justification, or at least without adequate justification. Moreover, it will become the focus of all of their attention and generate feelings that will fuel reactive conduct on their part and, in turn, on the part of their husband or wife. It will become a viscous cycle. That is always what happens in unhappy marriages. In time, as these actions and reactions play themselves out, husbands and wives no longer find themselves relating to the person they thought they married. Rather, they find themselves relating to a very different person.

Let me give you an example of this. A man who originally thought he had married a very organized woman now finds that he is married to a wife who is compulsive, not organized. In time, the husband who related in an appropriate manner to his wife whom he thought was organized, begins to relate very differently to his wife whom he now feels is compulsive. In fact, as his irritation over her compulsiveness increases, he begins to pick on her for no reason at all, or to pick on her excessively even when he does have a reason. Unfortunately, his wife, who happens to be a bit compulsive, now finds herself married, not to the nice man whom she thought she had married, but to a husband who picks on her for no reason at all, or at least for no apparent reason. Since she cannot understand why he is picking on her, and in the hope that this will assuage his upset, she responds by trying to show increased affection towards him. However, because he is angry with her, her husband does not respond to her demonstrations of affection as she would like and even rebuffs them. Since his wife does not understand why her good intentions have been ignored and rebuffed, she is understandably hurt and upset. Nor is her husband entirely unmindful of this since, underneath his irritation, he is basically a decent person. Nevertheless, because of his own upset and consequent anger, he has a very limited ability to respond to his wife's overtures which, on one level at least, anger him (because they do not address the underlying problem), but which, on another level, also leave him feeling somewhat guilty (because his wife does not know why her kindness is being repaid in that manner). In short, in time each of them is living out a very different marriage to a very different husband and wife from the one they married.

There is a moral in this. It is that our misunderstanding of how it is and why it is that marriages end in divorce causes us to respond inappropriately. It leads us to make judgments. Judgments may be appropriate in the face of a crime. They are not, however, when what we are confronted with is a tragedy. In those instances, silence, the suspension of judgments, is the more appropriate response. And let there be no mistake, divorce is a tragedy.

CHAPTER 4

RED LIGHTS AND GREEN LIGHTS

Husbands and wives stay married for very different reasons than they get married.

You have decided to get a divorce. You have even told your husband or wife this many times. But they do not hear you or pay any attention to you. In fact, they completely ignore you.

This has left you with a problem. You do not want to have to start the Third World War to get their attention. Your divorce is going to be difficult enough as it is. Nevertheless, you are not able to get them to take you seriously. You certainly cannot get their cooperation. Nor do you know where to turn or what to do. God knows you have told them often enough how unhappy you are, and that something has to change. You may have even mentioned separating and perhaps divorce. But they don't seem to hear you, or they don't want to, which is very much the same thing. What are you to do?

Let us consider this. Why don't they hear you? There are two reasons. The first and most obvious is that they do not like your message. They don't like the conclusion you have come to about your marriage. That does not mean that they do not have some complaints of their own. They do. After all, it is not possible for you to be as unhappy as you are and for them to be perfectly happy. They would certainly be happier if you wouldn't complain so much. Nevertheless, they don't want a divorce. They are not even able to think about it. Thus, if they hear you, particularly if they respond to you, they are going to end up where they do not want to be. Better not to hear you.

The second reason may surprise you. You have not been sending them a clear message, at least one as clear as you think you have. On the contrary, you have been sending out mixed signals.

Let me explain this. People stay married for very different reasons than they get married. They get married because they think that they are going to be blissfully happy, or at least happy forever. Nevertheless, they stay married even when they are not. Why do they do this? Because while their unhappiness may be pulling them away from their marriage, there are other things that are holding them to it. In other words, the considerations at play are not just in one direction.

You have been in that state for a long time now. There have been many things pulling you away from your marriage. Nevertheless, there have been other things that have held you to it. The proof of this is how long it has taken you to make the decision, despite how unhappy you have been for so long.

Although you are probably not aware of it, you have been sending out signals to your husband or wife throughout this time. That is not the problem. The problem is that you have been sending out mixed signals. When your terrible unhappiness got the upper hand and pulled you away from your marriage, the signal you sent out was a red light. That light said, "This has to stop. This marriage must end." Then, as time went by, you were not completely sure. As unhappy as you may have been, there were things that still held you to your marriage. When those considerations surfaced and momentarily ruled the day, as they occasionally did, the signal you sent out was a different one. It was a green light. It said, "Well, maybe."

To be sure, you sent out far more red lights than green ones. In fact, there have been ten times as many red ones. They have also been brighter and clearer. Nevertheless, there have been green ones, even if they have been few and far between.

What did those red lights and green lights tell your husband or wife? Remember, as bad as things were, they still did not want a divorce. They told them not to take you seriously. They told them that, despite all your complaints (all the red lights), if they waited long enough, a green one (or at least one that they could interpret as being green) would eventually come along. Up until now you have not disappointed them. To be sure, that is not how you see it. But that is how they see it.

What does this tell you? Two things. First, if you want your husband or wife to listen to you and to take you seriously, you are going to have to be consistent. You can't say "Stop" one day and "Well, maybe" the next.

It also tells you something else. To be sure, you have told them over and over again how you feel. But talk doesn't count. That is why they are not listening. They aren't watching your mouth (what you say). They are watching your feet (what you do), and that is your problem. For while your mouth may be saying one thing (that you are leaving), your feet are saying something else (that you are staying just where you are). Again, those are the mixed signals—the red lights and green lights—that you have been sending out.

To be sure, you will be able to give many good reasons to explain this. The first is that you don't want to be cruel. You know that this is very difficult for your husband or wife, and you do not want to make it any more difficult than it has to be. The second, as I said, is that you do not want to start the Third World War. At its best, divorce is never pleasant. But that doesn't mean that it makes any sense to make a nightmare of it. The third is that you have not been sure. You have hoped against hope that things might just get better and that you could avoid having to get a divorce.

Let us consider the first of those reasons—that you don't want to be cruel. You are right, there is never any occasion to be cruel. Ironically, however, sending out mixed signals to your husband or wife has not been kind either. In fact, it has been a little bit like a well known torture. That torture is the act of presenting different realities to a prisoner on different days. One day you are solicitous of his well-being and offer him a cigarette or some other courtesy. The next day you interrogate him for hours on end, insist that he give a false confession, and send veiled threats that he will be tortured into the confession if he does not give it voluntarily. The next day you treat him kindly again.

In most instances, we can adapt to the world that we live in, so long as it is consistent—so long as we know what world we are living in. What we cannot do, however, is adapt to an uncertain world, at least one that is radically uncertain—one that is kind one day and cruel the next. Thus, sending out mixed signals—red lights one day that tell your husband or wife all is lost, and green ones the next day that say, "Well maybe not," thereby reviving their hope (or at least allowing them to continue to indulge in the fantasy that all is still well)—is not really doing them any favor. It may not be cruel in the sense that it allays their fears, but nor is it kind, since their fears are well founded.

Let us consider the second reason. You are right in saying that you do not want your divorce to get out of hand and become more difficult than it has to be. Unfortunately, although you certainly have some control over that—you can avoid throwing the first stone—you cannot control it completely. For better or worse, your husband or wife is going to have a lot to do with that.

Nor is there any reason to believe that the tack you have been taking (holding back from pushing the matter too far) will ultimately prevent your worst fears from becoming a reality. All that you may have done is postpone the inevitable. In fact, it is even possible that it may end up leaving you where you do not want to be. Whether it is true or not, you have led your husband or wife to believe that if he or she holds out, and is patient, you may change your mind—change a red light to a green one. Who is to say what their attitude will be when they eventually learn that their own strategy has been for nought—that despite their patience and their perseverance, they are only to be left with what they want least and fear most. You can not know this—know that the tack you have taken is the right one.

This brings me to the last reason—that things may get better and that you may not be forced to divorce. When all is said and done, all this means is that you cannot predict the future—you can't be sure. That is the same philosophy that is used to sell lottery tickets. As they say, "Hey, you never know." But the fact that you cannot prove that things may not get better doesn't mean that you have any reason to believe they will. On the contrary, the idea that things just might get better goes against all of your experience, which tells you that they will only stay the same.

Making a decision under conditions such as this is simply to make a decision without all of the available information—without knowing what tomorrow will bring. But there is nothing unusual in this. That is the case with literally all of the decisions we make in our lives—that we are required to make those decisions with less than adequate information. That was true in your marriage. Why should it be any less true in your divorce?

Ironically, however, in most instances we know all that we need to know to make the decision. Put another way, there is really nothing that we are going to learn tomorrow that will put us in a better position to make the decision. That is because there is nothing that we are going to learn tomorrow that we do not know today.

Think about it. You are not being asked to decide whether the stock market will go up or down, or what interest rates will be a year from now. You would need a crystal ball to know that. The question you must answer is whether your husband or wife will change—be different tomorrow than he or she is today. But you do not need a crystal ball to answer that. They are not going to change because they do not know how to change. More to the point, they are not going to change because they do not want to change. In fact, they are quite happy being just who they are. If proof be needed, it is in the fact that you have threatened to divorce them again and again unless they change. Nevertheless, though the last thing they want is a divorce, they have still been unwilling (unable; it is one and the same thing) to do that.

What that means is that tomorrow will not be any different from today. There is therefore no need to wait for tomorrow. Nor is there any point in it, since you know all that you need to know today. Your problem, in other words, is not in what you know and do not know. Your problem is taking the first step and acting on what you know.

What is the first step? As difficult as it is, it is still simple. If you want your husband or wife to accept the reality that the marriage is over, you will have to present them with a consistent reality, not inconsistent realities that contradict one another. Again, I am not suggesting that you be unfeeling, let alone cruel. I am just suggesting that you be consistent.

CHAPTER 5

THE OTHER PARTY

People do not want to change. They are quite happy being who they are.

If you are the one who does not want a divorce, things are going to appear very different. In fact, you will probably not be able to understand it at all—not understand why you are getting a divorce in the first place. You may even think that your husband or wife is making a terrible mistake. You will certainly want them to reconsider it. For the same reason, you will be upset that they are prepared to end the marriage without first trying to save it. Even if there have been such efforts in the past that did not prove successful, you may still feel that the two of you should try one more time.

As is so often the case, you may even be stunned by your wife's or husband's decision. You literally didn't see it coming. Of course there were problems. What marriage doesn't have problems? But nothing that serious—certainly not anything serious enough to justify a divorce.

I know that what I am going to say will be very difficult for you to hear let alone accept, but the truth is that if you did not see it coming it is because you were not paying close attention. For years now, your husband or wife has been waving their hands in the air, signaling just how unhappy they were and begging you to change. In fact, from their standpoint, they do not know what more they could have done to get your attention. If they have now finally decided to get a divorce, it is simply because they are so worn down that they have given up trying.

In fairness, it is not all your fault. You didn't see because you didn't want to see. If you had seen—if you had really understood their complaint—you would have had to change. But you didn't want to change. You were quite happy being who you are. Nor would you have known how to change. That is why it was easier not to see. That is also why this is such a surprise to you, and why you didn't see it coming. You were hoping that it would just go away.

If the truth be told, it is not anyone's fault. In most cases at least, no one really did anything so terrible. You didn't rob a bank. You don't steal candy from children. In fact, if you are guilty of anything, it is simply in being who you are, which is obviously no crime at all. To be sure, you have your faults and limitations. Who doesn't? But people don't get divorced because they are good people or bad people. They get divorced, as I said, because they are different people and because, over time, those differences begin to rub against one another and create serious friction.

Unfortunately, if you are the one who does not want the divorce, it will be very difficult, if not impossible, for you to see this. To do that, you would have to be able to see your husband's or wife's complaint, and you are not able to do that. In fact, from your standpoint, it is their constant complaining that is the problem in the marriage, and if they would only stop, there wouldn't be any problem, or at least any serious one.

Nor, unfortunately, will anything that I might say be of very much help to you. That is because your loss is too great. That is because you are too hurt and angry. That is because all of your attention is focused on your husband's or wife's actions. That is because your whole world seems to be coming apart.

What are you to do? In one sense, of course, there is not very much that you can do. You will certainly not be able to change how your husband or wife feels. Maybe that might have been possible before, but it is highly unlikely now. As is so often the case when couples get to this point, it is too little too late. All that you can do, therefore, is look to yourself. You must somehow find the way to accept something that it is not possible for you to understand.

I admit that this is asking a great deal of you. Nor is it something that anyone can do for you. Nevertheless, I would like to try to be of some help. Understandably, you are struggling with some very difficult feelings. In part, those feelings serve to protect you by coming to your defense. The problem is that you will do more than hold on to those feelings for support. There is the danger that you will also savor them. If you do that, they will become a liability rather than an asset. That is because they will be a crutch that you will be unable to walk without. That is because they will cause you to look back rather than to look forward.

What can you do to make it easier for you to let go of those difficult feelings? One thing would be to try to look to the future. Unfortunately, there is a problem in that. The future is never clear let alone certain. In a sense it is just an abstraction. It is therefore not solid enough to hold onto or to sustain you. You will therefore have to find something more concrete.

There is something that will better serve your purpose. It is not possible for your husband or wife to have been as unhappy as they claim and for you to have been perfectly happy. Rather, to maintain the relationship, you had to make compromises as well. More likely than not, you were even forced to make sacrifices.

Understandably, you have avoided looking at these compromises. To have acknowledged them would have forced you to ask questions that you were not prepared to ask. Nevertheless, those questions were there. You just didn't want to see them. It might make sense for you to look at them now and acknowledge the reality that your marriage didn't meet important needs of yours as well. Seeing that might make it easier for you to let go of the past and to look to the future.

I do not want to be misunderstood here. I am not suggesting that what has happened to you is really a blessing in disguise. That would be worse than nonsense. It would be irresponsible. I am only saying that, as good as your reasons may have been for holding onto your marriage, you were nevertheless required to pay a price to do that. Nor am I suggesting that you look back in anger. Rather, I am trying to give you a way to combat the difficult feelings you are struggling with that are fueling that anger. That is to balance the weight of those feelings with the realization that your marriage wasn't meeting certain essential needs of yours as well. That realization may just make it possible for you to let go of those feelings that are causing you to look back rather than forward.

I must tell you something else. There is a price to be paid if you are unable to hear your husband or wife. By definition, you are where you are because he or she has drawn a line and said that your marriage must end, or at least that the two of you must separate. That leaves you only one choice: since you cannot go back, you can only go forward. Unfortunately, if you cannot go forward with your husband or wife, you will leave them no option. They will be forced to go forward without you.

It is not in your best interests for this to happen. It is not in anyone's best interests. This will be difficult enough as it is. There is no point in making it any more difficult. Remember, the only thing worse than a bad marriage is a terrible divorce.

CHAPTER 6

LOOKING OUTSIDE OF THE MARRIAGE

Most of what passes for sex has nothing to do with sex.

Not uncommonly, husbands and wives who are desperately unhappy will look outside their marriage for emotional support. Thirty or forty years ago, this was far more common of men than it was of women. Today it is very much the same for both.

I said, "look outside of their marriage for emotional support" rather than "have an affair." That is how I always refer to what has happened. It is not just that I do not wish to make moral judgments. When I see a marriage that has failed, and the terrible disappointment it has brought to everyone involved, what I see is a tragedy, not a crime. It is that the word "affair" is very loaded. More to the point, it really does not tell you very much. It tells you what happened, but not why. Again, it causes you to look at the wrong starting point.

Before I address this, however, I want to say that I think that these outside relationships are terribly unfortunate. In fact, if the person who becomes involved in such a relationship could see its consequences in advance, he or she would never enter into it. For the person whose husband or wife has formed such a relationship, it is nothing short of devastating. It is a mortal blow to their self-esteem. Worse, they cannot help but take it personally, as if it was intentionally directed at them. In fact, they will be unable to see it any other way.

Before things get to that point, it would be far better to

acknowledge just how bad your marriage is, get off the fence and make a decision. When someone does not do that (which is far too often the case), it is because the needs that the outside relationship fulfills, if only for the moment, are so pressing and its (seeming) satisfaction so overpowering that one's more critical faculties are dulled. In many instances, they do not function at all.

The problem is that these relationships are not formed in this way. Someone does not say to himself or herself that they have a pressing need and then look to satisfy it. To be sure, the other party to the marriage, who will be the one on the receiving end, will not be able to see this, let alone accept it. Nevertheless, husbands and wives do not plan to have these outside relationships. They just happen. Your common sense will tell you that. Someone who becomes emotionally involved with his or her next-door neighbor wasn't planning for this to happen. If they were, they would have picked someone on the far end of town, or five towns away, not their co-worker, a neighbor or, worst of all, a close friend of their spouse. No, the thing that most distinguishes the other person is simply the fact that he or she was there.

What causes people to violate everything that their common sense would tell them and form these relationships? It is that, if someone is desperately unhappy in his or her marriage, as people who contemplate divorce are, their husband or wife is no longer able to fulfill a very important need of theirs—to make them feel like a man or a woman. In fact, they have not felt that in a very long time, and they desperately need to. For better or worse, we are brought up that way. That is why people look outside their marriage. To be sure, sex may be the medium of exchange, but it is not really the commodity being exchanged. (Though we do not appreciate this as we should, most of what passes for sex has little to do with sex.) What the other person is able to do, at least for the moment—and this may really be his or her only virtue—is enable the unhappy party to feel something that they have a desperate need to feel, but that they have not felt in a very long time.

Unfortunately, both the husband or wife involved in the outside relationship and his or her spouse will put far too much significance in it, one, because they will overvalue it and the other because it represents such a mortal blow to their sense of themselves that they can only see it as an act of betrayal.

Why do I say that the person involved in the outside relationship will overvalue it? Because, in most instances, it is only a bridge relationship formed by one very unhappy person and someone who is either flattered by the attention or who is acting out a rescue fantasy. Or, as is more often the case, it is formed by two kindred souls, each of whom senses a similar need in the other. That is their common bond—that they are both locked in unhappy marriages. Ultimately, it may also prove to be the only thing they have in common. Nevertheless, since it is a lot easier for someone to leave something for something else than to leave it for nothing, many unhappy husbands and wives look to these outside relationships as life-savers. But there is a problem. While the relationship may give them the strength to let go of their failed marriage, once they have done that, all too often they find that they do not have anything of substance to hold onto—that the relationship does not have enough staying power on its own. Aside from the terrible pain and humiliation this relationship will cause to their husband or wife—and be there no misunderstanding, it will—in more instances than not, it will only prove to have been fools gold. To be sure, it will not feel that way when it is in full bloom. But when the bloom fades, as it all too often does, it will.

There is something else that must be said about these outside relationships that will cause no end of pain to the person on the receiving end. That is the fact that they will necessarily involve deceit. If you are the one involved in the relationship, you are obviously not going to announce it to your husband or wife. Rather you are going to keep it to yourself. There are many reasons for this. The obvious one is that, at least in the beginning, you do not know where, if at all, the relationship is going. Even if you do know, however, what would be the point in telling your husband or wife? Just to bring them up to date on what is going on in your life? Just to be truthful? Telling the truth may make sense as a general rule. But there are exceptions, particularly if the truth is going to hurt someone other than yourself. After all, for whose benefit would you be telling the truth, yours or your spouse's?

There are other reasons why you may not want to make the relationship public. You may not be ready for the consequences of making it public. You may feel guilty. But even if these were not considerations enough, there is more. There are other people involved. There is the other person's spouse, who may not know and who, for the same reasons, the other person does not want to know. There is the community. And of course, there are your children.

Even if you decide to keep the relationship under wraps, however, it is not going to be easy. While your husband or wife may not know about it from the start, in time they may come to sense it. There will be little things of which you are not even aware that will give it away. There will be changes in your attitude. There will be changes in your conduct. You will have to explain your actions and your absences. In short, excuses will have to be made. Each lie will require another lie. In time there will be such a house of lies that it will crumble of its own weight. Your husband or wife will then have to deal with the double deceit—the deceit of your relationship and your deceit in hiding it and then in lying about it.

There is one final word that must be said about the relationships that desperately unhappy husbands and wives form outside of their marriage. Sometimes they are just pleas for help. It is not that the party is consciously using the relationship to send out a message to his or her spouse. Certainly that is not how their husband or wife will see it. It is just that, in many instances at least, the party who forms the relationship really has no intention of leaving the marriage, at least no present intention. It is just a desperate act on his or her part within the context of the marriage. The problem is that it quickly gets out of hand and develops a life of its own.

The one thing that can be said for certain about these relationships is that it will make any future attempt by the two of you to address the problems in your marriage (or divorce) exponentially more difficult, if not impossible. That will certainly be the case if your husband or wife learns of the relationship, which they commonly will. (To be more accurate, they may not learn of it if they do not want to know about it, but they will learn of it when they finally do.) To begin with, it will just add one more problem to what is already an overburdened situation. But it will do something else. By definition, if you are the one who is desperately unhappy in the marriage and who has formed the relationship, you will have a long list of grievances, and if the two of you finally seek counseling, you will want to put them on the table at the outset. But you will never get a chance. That is because your husband or wife, who has been so devastated by the relationship, will want to put their issues on the table first. In fact, they will not even want to hear anything else.

Thus, while there may be some momentary satisfaction in these relationships, there is little profit in them. Rarely, if ever, do they make things better. They only make things worse. That is why I said that they are so terribly unfortunate, and that you owe it to your husband or wife, and to yourself, to make a decision about your marriage before things get to this point. As you would not be able to live with the humiliation that this will inflict, neither will your husband or wife.

That is why the better counsel is to make one decision at a time—make the decision to end one relationship before you make a decision to enter another. As any mental health professional will tell you, it is always better not to make important decisions in your life when you are in a state of great emotional turmoil or when you are going through a major life transition. And short of the death of a child or someone else extremely close to you, ending your marriage is about as great an emotional upheaval as you are likely to encounter in your life.

Again, I am not saying any of this to pass judgment or to shame anyone. I know how someone who is drowning in his or her marriage feels. I therefore understand what causes them to look outside their marriage. All that I am saying is that there is inevitably a price to be paid and that in the end, the piper will demand to be paid.

PART II

Personal Choices

CHAPTER 7

STAYING IN CONTROL

If you do not take control of the events in your life,
the events in your life will take control of you.

Without question, divorce is overwhelming. That is why people run off to the library and to the bookstore to read as much as they can about it. That is also why they talk to as many people as they do. They want to prepare themselves. Prepare themselves for what? Ironically, for the nightmare that they will unwittingly make of their divorce if they are not careful.

They will read books that tell them that it is a crazy time. They will read others that will suggest they can grow through the experience. They will even read some that will tell them how to have a good divorce or a spiritual divorce. And, of course, they will read no end of books that tell them what to do and what not to do, though they really do not understand what they are being told, and are often too emotionally overwhelmed even to hear it. Finally, they will seek out books that will tell them what their legal rights are (though never what their legal obligations are) and, most important, how to go about finding a good lawyer, which usually means finding a tough one. What these books will not tell them, of course, is that the only thing a tough lawyer will do is make their divorce even tougher than it has to be.

Unfortunately, most people are just as confused when they get through as they were when they began. Reading all those books did not help. All that they did was reinforce their fear, and their feeling that they were lost and adrift at sea. All that they did was convince them that what they needed was someone to protect them. All that they did was send them off in the wrong direction.

I am sure that you do not want to make your life any more difficult than it already is. I am therefore not going to fill your head with a lot of useless information or prepare you for your worst nightmare. And I am not going to suggest that, like the proverbial chicken with its head cut off, you run off in a hundred different directions going nowhere. To be sure, that may cause you to think that you are doing something, but you are not. It is only an illusion.

My counsel is going to be very different. It is also going to be so simple that you cannot possibly mistake it. It is that you must stop, think, and use your common sense. You must act sensibly rather than just react emotionally. Most important, you must remember this. If you do not take control of the events in your life, the events in your life will take control of you. At all costs, you cannot afford to let that happen.

At its best, divorce is never easy. But that does not mean that you should make it any more difficult than it has to be. Ironically, the choice is yours. It will be as hard as the two of you make it. You can get through it in one piece or you can end up in pieces.

There is a lesson in this. As we all know from experience, the success of a marriage is not a function of how much someone spent on their wedding or how much time went into its planning. One has nothing to do with the other. The same is true of divorce. You can make this a very big and costly affair if you wish. But that does not mean that it will come out any different. It certainly won't come out better. It will just take that much longer and cost that much more to get there.

There is no profit in that. Unlike a wedding, no one looks back on their divorce with fond memories. It is anything but a pleasant experience. That is why there is no point in letting it get out of control.

CHAPTER 8

THE TWO OF US TOGETHER, OR EACH OF US ON OUR OWN

A marriage is about two people.
A divorce is about two people as well.

I said that it is critical that you stay in control rather than allow the events in your life take control of you. What can cause that to happen?

There are a number of things. While marriage is about "the two of us" together, it is natural to see divorce as being about "you" and "me" individually. In truth, it was "you" and "me" in your marriage as well. After all, you did not marry your husband or wife as an act of charity. It was something that you did for yourself.

Nevertheless, there is a difference. While you were two different people in your marriage as you now are in your divorce, you were both going in the same general direction. The fact of your marriage and, more importantly, your desire to maintain it, tended to keep in check, at least to some extent, the differences in "you" and "me" in the name of "us." In other words, it tended to act as a restraint preventing things from getting too far out of control.

Now that you are divorcing, however, that has dramatically changed. It is no longer the "two of us." It is just "you" and "me," or so it seems. Worse, you will not only be told by one and all to think only of yourself, but also to go your own way and seek your own counsel. Unfortunately, what no one will tell you is that that is always how things get out of hand.

There is only one way to prevent that from happening. That is to acknowledge that this is still something the two of you have to do together. In fact, that is the simple message of this book. The two of you can either go off together and work with one another, or you can each go off on your own, resort to self help, and work against one another. That is your choice.

If you follow the understanding that you must not let the events in your lives take control of you, there can only be one choice. Despite your divorce, and despite the hurt and misunderstanding that are its inevitable by-product, the two of you are locked in a common enterprise and have a common cause. That common enterprise is to bring your marriage to a conclusion and that common cause is to do it in such a way that it does not get out of control and become the Third World War. Running off in different directions and resorting to self help (hiring separate lawyers to be your champions) will not change that. It will just cause you to lose sight of it. For better or worse, your husband or wife is your reality. He or she will not go away. It is therefore only a question of how you will deal with each other. You can work with one another, or you can each go off on your own, resort to self help, and work against one another. That is your choice, and all the rest is just talk.

I said that the two of you are locked in a common enterprise and have a common cause. The common enterprise is your need to sit down and make all of the practical decisions that are incident to your divorce. Those practical decisions can involve such simple things as deciding who will keep the teapot and the lawn furniture, to the more complicated questions of what will happen to your home, the proceeds in your savings account, and your retirement benefits. If you have children or if you have been married for a considerable period, that common enterprise will become more complicated. It will be to determine how each of you will be able to manage financially in the future and the obligation, if any, that one of you should have to the other, and to your children, to be concerned with how they will be able to do that.

While you may be able to recognize the common enterprise, it may be more difficult to see the common cause. Nor is this something that anyone else will point out to you. It is not to allow your limited self-interests (as to who will keep the lawn furniture or even the proceeds in your savings account) to undermine the more important interests that you still have in common.

What are your common interests? If you have children, they are obviously one of them. But you have others, as well. Principal amongst those is not to allow your self-interests (what divorce lawyers call your "conflicting interests") to get so out of hand that they will do violence to your overall best interests. And it is not in your overall best interests to take what is already a great tragedy in your life and turn it into a nightmare. Again, that is just common sense. Nevertheless, that is what will happen if you let the events in your life take control of you. That is what will happen if you go off on your own and employ a procedure that, in leaving you feeling vulnerable, will necessarily encourage you to resort to self help.

CHAPTER 9

THE TWO ROADS

The only thing worse then a bad marriage
is a terrible divorce.

As you will find, you are at a critical fork. There are two different roads you can go down. I have been down both of them in my professional life. I know where each of them leads. I also know the terrible price that divorcing husbands and wives pay when they go down the wrong one.

If you go down one of those roads, you will not go off together. Rather, you will each go off on your own. That is the road where you will each resort to self help. That is the road where each of you will look out only for himself and herself, and neither of you will have any concern for what will happen to the other. That is the road where you will work against one another. That is the road where the rule will be that there are no rules, that it is anything that the law will allow—really, anything that the law will let you get away with. That is the road you will go down if you each go off and retain separate lawyers. That road is known as an adversarial divorce proceeding.

The other road is the one you will go down if you go off together. It is the one you will take if you want to be the ones who will make the important decisions in your lives rather than to turn those decisions over to others. It is the road you will take if you are trying to make some sense of what is happening to you rather than to make a game out of it. It is the one you will take if you want to control the events in your life rather than let the events in your life take control of you. Most importantly, it is the road you will take if you want to conclude an agreement that works for both of you, not just for one of you at the expense of the other. And since you will be going off together, you will retain the services of one person to help you rather than two. That road is known as divorce mediation.

Having traveled down both of those roads in my professional life, I can tell you that there is only one rational choice. Not that the road I am recommending is a wonderful road. Since there is nothing wonderful about divorce, it would be irresponsible for me to suggest that. On the contrary, it can be a bit bumpy. Why then do I recommend it? Because there is light at the end of that road. Because it does not take forever or cost a king's ransom. Because it does not take on a life of its own. Because it is the better of the two. The road I am recommending may be uncertain; the other is a certain disaster. It is a blind alley. You will only get lost if you go down it.

Why then do divorcing husbands and wives so often make the mistake of going down that road? There are many reasons, but the principal one is that they buy into legal mythology. They buy into the rather strange idea that lawyers know what is best for them. They also buy into the equally strange idea that lawyers will somehow protect them. The truth, of course, is just the opposite. Having gone off on their own, retained separate lawyers and resorted to self help, they will now each need protection.

They buy into legal mythology in another way as well. They allow it to persuade them that turning to lawyers and allowing them to make the important decisions in their lives is a perfectly natural thing to do. It isn't. It is very unnatural. If proof be needed, it is in the fact that they would never have thought to do that before.

Nevertheless, they buy into it anyway. One reason is that the first step seems such a small one. All that they are doing is going to get some information and to ask some questions. What they do not see, of course, is that it only takes one step. That is because what they are stepping onto is a moving walkway that has a momentum of its own. By the time they realize this, however, it is too late. By that time it will be almost impossible for them to get off. That is because they will have violated the cardinal rule. They will have turned over the decisions in their lives to others. They will have allowed the events in their lives to take control of them.

This, then, is your choice. You can go off together and work with one another, or you can each go off on your own, resort to self-help, and work against one another. It is that simple, and if anyone presents it to you in any other terms, it is because they do not want you to see this.

Unfortunately, it will be presented to you in other terms. To blind you to this simple choice, those who will urge you to go off on your own will do two things. First, they will invoke lofty abstractions and talk about what is "fair" and "just" and "right." Second, they will play to your fear. They will do that because lofty abstractions and fear always play well.

I must warn you that these will be extremely persuasive arguments. Since you cannot help but feel that a terrible wrong has been done to you in your marriage, all of the talk about what is fair and right and just will necessarily resonate with you. And since you cannot help but feel frightened by the prospect of your divorce, all of the talk about protection will give you comfort.

You cannot allow yourself to be taken in by any of this. You cannot allow your fear and the siren call of these lofty abstractions take your eye off the mark. That is what causes divorcing husbands and wives to go down the wrong road. That is what causes them to end up getting lost.

CHAPTER 10

THE SELF-FULFILLING PROPHECY

What you see is what you will get.

If the two of you go off on your own, resort to self help and initiate an adversarial divorce proceeding, you will necessarily buy into something. Before you do that, it is important that you know what that is.

As you know, our legal system is an adversarial one. Nor do lawyers apologize for that. Rather, they are very proud of it. Why did we create an adversarial legal system? Because we assumed that those who turned to it would be adversaries. If we thought they would be friends, we would have created a friendly system. But it is not a friendly system, as anyone who has employed it will tell you.

But aren't the two of you adversaries? It makes no difference. Whether you are adversaries, whether you wish to be adversaries, or whether it makes any rational sense for you to become adversaries, in assuming that you are, and in then organizing you as adversaries, like every self-fulfilling prophecy, that is exactly what you will become.

A self-fulfilling prophecy is something that becomes true because we believe it to be true. Because you are divorcing, you believe that your husband or wife is your adversary. That assumption is going to leave you feeling vulnerable and put you on your guard. Viewing you as an adversary, as well, your spouse is going to feel the same. In time, one of you will feel the need to resort to self-help and to take some pre-emptive action to protect yourself against the threat that you perceive the other to be. The other will return the compliment and resort to self help as well. For each "tit" there will be a "tat", *ad infinitum*. In time you will both have all the proof you need that the other can not be trusted. By then you really will be adversaries. That is how the self-fulfilling prophecy always works when you resort to self help, retain separate lawyers and commit yourself to legal warfare. Don't be fooled. Notwithstanding all the lofty abstractions that lawyers love to invoke about what is fair and right and just, that is exactly what you will be doing. The self-fulfilling prophecy is just the glue that will bind you to that commitment when those abstractions begin to lose their luster and their power begins to fade.

Just the opposite will be the case if the two of you go down the other road together. To be sure, there is a self-fulfilling prophecy at work there as well. But it plays out very differently. That is because it does not proceed on the assumption that the two of you are adversaries and then organize you as adversaries. Because you will not be organized in that manner, you will not begin to act as adversaries. There will be no need to; nor will there be any point in it.

When I meet with a couple for the first time, I employ a simple metaphor to underscore how those different self-fulfilling prophecies will play out in each of those settings. The three of us are sitting at a small round table in the conference room in my office. Placing my hands face down on the table, I tell them that if they employ my services, we are always going to meet with one another with our hands on top of the table. Neither of them is going to have to worry what took place at the last meeting when they were not there. There was no such meeting. If one of them asks me a question, I want the other to be there to hear the answer. It is hands on top of the table.

That is not how they will meet if they each go off on their own, however. Removing my hands from the table and placing them underneath it, I tell them that, in that setting, it will be hands under the table, and even if my hands aren't doing anything, it will still make them very nervous that they are not able to see them.

It is important that you remember this. If you each go off on your own and retain separate lawyers, the two of you are not going to meet openly with your hands on top of the table. Rather, you will meet with your hands under the table. In other words, you will each meet with your own attorney secretly, privately, behind closed doors. Even though you will be the principal topic of conversation when your husband or wife meets with his or her attorney, no invitation will be extended to you. In fact, should you learn of the meeting and decide to attend, they will feel very uncomfortable by your presence and the meeting will quickly adjourn.

What are you to think? There is only one thing that you can think: that they are meeting to plan and to plot. To be sure, what they are planning for you may be a surprise. But it will not be a surprise party. What are you to do? There is really only one thing you can do, and that is to go off and get a lawyer yourself. That, of course, is how the self-fulfilling prophecy works when you resort to self help and retain separate lawyers. That is always how things get out of control.

To be sure, that is not how a divorce lawyer will describe what is taking place. Rather, to justify his or her conduct, he will again sprinkle legal holy water on it and invoke lofty abstractions. What he will say is that being able to meet secretively, privately, behind closed doors with your own attorney is one of the great virtues of our adversarial legal system. He even has a name for it. He calls it "confidentiality." What he will not tell you, and what the abstractions he employs will obscure, is that what our adversarial legal system is doing is encouraging each of you to go off and tell secrets to your respective attorneys, adding "Don't tell my wife. Don't tell my husband."

Of necessity, your divorce raises very important questions that the two of you must address and answer. As such, it is serious business, far too serious to make a game of it. Ballparks are for people who want to play games. Sitting down together with your hands on top of the table is for people who want to make some sense of their situation, as much as they can. The lofty abstractions that lawyers invariably invoke will not change that. All that they will do is prevent you from being able to see it.

CHAPTER 11

CONTEXT

Context is everything. To be sure, it will not change a lion into a lamb.
But it can prevent a lamb from feeling that it is necessary to act like a lion

I said that our adversarial legal system works on the basis of a self-fulfilling prophecy. The technical term for this is context, and context is everything. Context will not change a lion into a lamb. But even lions and lambs act differently in different contexts. If you do not believe me, go over to a sleeping lion and awaken it.

It is not possible to understand this if, like a divorce lawyer, all your experience takes place in the adversarial world of divorce. You will see how divorcing husbands and wives act as being an inevitable part of divorce itself rather than of the particular world of divorce that you happen to be in.

The same was true of me. When my professional life was that of an adversarial divorce lawyer, I assumed that all divorcing husbands and wives acted as inappropriately as did those whom I encountered. What else was I to think? It was the only world I knew. It was only when I decided to go down the other road, and found myself in a very different world, that I came to appreciate the importance of context. What was so different? The fact that I literally never had to deal with all of the brush fires that continually ignite when husbands and wives each go off on their own. These fires just didn't start when the two of them went off together.

What are these brush fires? They are the terribly inappropriate and counterproductive conduct that divorcing husbands and wives invariably engage in when they turn to adversarial divorce proceedings. They are the acts of self-help that they each feel compelled to resort to in a context in which, since there are no rules (since it is anything that the law will allow), they do not know what to expect from the other. That is why they feel the need to resort to self-help.

It can start with one of the parties canceling the credit cards that the other is using or going to the bank and withdrawing the proceeds in their joint savings account. It can end with one of them getting a notice that the electric service will be disconnected or the mortgage on their home foreclosed, or with the other arriving to pick up his children for the weekend only to find that they are not there. However it starts, for every action there will be a reaction. However it starts, in time no one will be able to remember how it began.

Again, legal mythology would have you believe that divorcing husbands and wives retain separate lawyers because they will protect them. What no one will tell you is that it is the very context in which those proceedings take place that will cause you to need protection. There is something else that you will not be told, and that is that it is a lot easier to start those brush fires than it is to put them out. Again, that is because adversarial divorce proceedings get out of control and take on a life of their own. What is the moral of the story? It is that you can put yourselves in a context that will not cause the two of you to feel that it is either necessary or appropriate to engage in such conduct, or you can put yourselves in a context in which you will be forced to deal with such conduct. That is your choice.

Let me give you an example of this. Sometime ago, I was working with a couple where some of these fears began to surface. As is usually the case, the decision to divorce had been made by one of them, in this instance the husband. At our first working meeting, he announced that it was his intention to leave his and his wife's home shortly and establish a separate residence for himself. He wanted to put this on the table so that there would be no surprises. While I sensed that his wife had no objection to this, nevertheless, as he spoke, I could see that she was becoming somewhat anxious. Wishing to address her concern, I turned to her and said: "I don't know why you are so worried. Your husband isn't abandoning you or your children. He is just establishing a separate residence for himself. The bills are still going to be paid as they have been in the past. He is not going to leave you high and dry. There is nothing for you to worry about. Yes, he will not be able to turn over his entire paycheck to you as he has in the past. But there are not going to be any abrupt changes. This isn't going to take forever. We are going to get it done in a relatively short period of time. You will then both know what you are supposed to do and what you can expect."

What was I doing? Obviously, assuaging the wife's fears. But I was doing something more. I was setting the ground rules. I was telling them (and particularly the husband) what I expected. What I expected was that there were not going to be any surprises.

I was doing one last thing. I was letting the husband know that I was aware that he could not hold his breath forever—in other words, pay all of the bills in the future just as he had in the past. After all, he would now have his own separate expenses as well. But I did not want any sudden changes. I did not want anything to distract us from the business at hand. They both heard me, their respective concerns had been addressed, and the discussions proceeded without further incident.

Are those the same ground rules that the husband's lawyer would have given him had the two of them gone off separately and resorted to self help? Obviously not. After all, his lawyer's concern would not be how the husband's wife or even his children would be able to manage in the future. Rather, his concern would be limited to his client (the husband) alone which, in the context here, would mean not to allow him to set a precedent by giving his wife what she needed. Thus, the ground rules that the husband's lawyer would have set would have been to give her as little as he could get away with (as little as the law would allow).

As this story indicates, context is not only important in terms of what it discourages. It is also important in terms of what it promotes. Let me give you another example to illustrate this. Admittedly, it is a little unusual.

Several years ago, I was working with a couple who had been married for about ten years. They had one daughter who at the time was about seven years of age. Again, the decision to divorce had been made by just one of them, in this instance the wife. It was a particularly difficult experience for the husband, who very much did not want the divorce, and he was very resistant to it. However, he found the setting in which his and his wife's discussions took place to be very supportive, it enabled him to begin to come to terms with the reality of his divorce, and they successfully concluded an agreement.

In this case, what took place occurred about two years later. I received a telephone call from the wife who told me that she and her former husband were having some serious disagreements with respect to their daughter. In fact, she said that when he had dropped off their daughter the night before, they had had a very heated discussion which ended very unpleasantly. I suggested that the two of them schedule an appointment so that we could discuss this together, and after speaking with him, she did that.

Since we had worked together before, I knew them quite well. When they arrived, to get re-acquainted and to break the ice, we talked for a few minutes about things in general before we got down to business. As is my custom, I let them do most of the talking. Within a very short time, the conversation had turned from a three-way discussion into a two-way conversation, just between the two of them. Since they were doing very well on their own and seemed to have no difficulty, I just sat there quietly, listening.

Some considerable period of time elapsed, during which the two of them sat there talking to one another without incident. In fact, their discussions were very civil. Though I listened carefully to everything they said, I did not say a word. It was almost as if I was not even in the room. At that point, and just as our time was beginning to run out, the husband turned to me and said, "This has been extremely helpful. Do you think that we could schedule another appointment?"

Am I suggesting that context acts as a truth serum or that it will change a lion into a lamb? I did not say that. I only wish it were that simple. What I am insisting, however, is that context is critical, and that it can often prevent a lamb from feeling the need to act like a lion.

CHAPTER 12

THE GREEK CHORUS

To mean well and to do well is not always one and the same thing.

Whenever husbands and wives get to this point in their lives, there arises around each of them a group of people whom I have given a name. I call them the "Greek Chorus of well-wishers." You may have already met them. These are the people who, from the sidelines, will give you information, give you advice, offer you encouragement and urge you on. They mean well. Of course they mean well. They are your friends and relatives. Nevertheless, to mean well and to do well is not one and the same thing. In fact, if there is ever a time when well-meaning people will invariably do more harm than good it is now.

There are many reasons for this. First, not everything you will be told will be true. On the contrary, half of it will be just the opposite. Your problem is that you will not know which is which. You will therefore tend to listen to all of it, the nonsense as well as the sense. Unfortunately, it is going to get you into a lot of trouble.

Let me be clear. This is not just what you will be told by friends and relatives. It is what you will be told by anyone who, from the sidelines, comments on what is going on. That includes clergymen, accountants and even lawyers. In fact, it never ceases to amaze me how much misinformation and mis-direction seemingly well meaning professionals give to husbands and wives considering divorce.

Second, what you will be told and what your husband or wife will be told will not be the same. (Think about it. If the two of you were told the same thing, you wouldn't have a problem in the first place.) In fact, what you will each be told will often be 180 degrees apart. Unfortunately, since you will never get to hear what your husband or wife was told, and since literally everyone who bends your ear will tell you very much the same thing, you will tend to believe it. Worse, you will accept it as gospel. Thus, if your husband or wife, based on what he or she has been told, expresses a different opinion, you will have no choice but to conclude that he or she is acting in bad faith. (Since you know the truth, what else could it be?) That will leave the two of you with a problem.

Third, your Greek Chorus will invariably underscore your worst fears. It is understandable that you are frightened, particularly if you are the one who is more financially dependent. You will now be going forward on your own, and you are naturally worried that you may not have enough. That is a real problem, and it is very anxiety-producing. But you do not need to be told what you already know. Nor do you need to be frightened even more than you already are. What you need is help. What you need is reassurance. That is what friends are for.

Fourth, your Greek Chorus will undermine your confidence. This is a very difficult time in your life. You are in a state of great emotional upset. The very structure of your life is being undermined. Understandably, you will tend to lose your bearings. At times like these, if we are smart, we will fall back on the bedrock of values we were brought up to believe in and that normally define who we are. In short, we will try to act as the decent, responsible people we like to think we are and that we would still like to be, despite what is happening to us. At least that is what we will do if we will think things through rather than allow ourselves to be carried away by our emotions.

If you were to do that at any other time in your life, you would probably get a pat on the back. If you were young enough, you might even have a little gold star pinned on you. If you were to do that now, however, you will not get the same encouragement. Rather, your Greek Chorus will unsettle you by knocking at your knees and undermining your confidence. "You mean to say that after what he or she did, you would be willing to do that? You must be a fool."

Despite your hurt, despite your anger, despite all of the other feelings that tend to overwhelm you, you would still very much like to do the right thing—be the person you were brought up to be. Your problem is that you are not sure whether, should you do this, you are being a hero or a fool. It is not that you need to be a hero; you just do not want to be left a fool. If there was any doubt in your mind, your Greek Chorus will now have resolved it.

Again, while your Greek Chorus may mean well, they are not doing you any favor. They have not told you this, but your only hope is that you do not lose control of the events in your life and allow them to take control of you. That is exactly what will happen, however, if you follow their advice, resort to self-help and go off on your own.

There is only one way to prevent this from happening, and that is to continue to act responsibly, as difficult as that will be. And it will be difficult. These are difficult times. That is why it is so important to think carefully rather than to follow your feelings wherever they lead—that you act rather than just react. If you do, you will end up lost. Remember, if anything goes—if it is each of you for himself or herself—then anything can happen. You cannot afford to let that happen. In fact, at no other time in your life would anyone give you advice as irresponsible as this. Nor would you listen to it.

Unfortunately, as bad as all of this is, there is more. The message that your Greek Chorus will implicitly send out to you is: "You can no longer look to him (or her). You can no longer trust him. You must look out for yourself." To be sure, it may not be possible for you to look to your husband or wife as you did in the past. But that does not mean that it makes any sense to turn him or her into your worst enemy. There is still a problem that the two of you have to sit down, address, and hopefully resolve. You still only have two choices. You can do that by working together, with one another, or you can do that by working on your own, against one another.

I must add something. Before I do, however, I must acknowledge that if you cannot help but see your divorce as a terrible injustice that has been done to you—as I would say, a crime rather than a tragedy—what I am about to tell you will not be very helpful. You will probably not even be able to hear it let alone accept it, and I apologize for that. Nevertheless, even if you are not able to hear it now, perhaps in time you will. What I am going to tell you is that, in an important sense, the two of you still need each other. True, you may be divorcing and going your own separate ways. But you still have had a life and a history and possibly children together. More important, you must both make some sense of what has happened to you, each in your own way. While neither of you can do that for the other, you can still help one another. How? By doing it together. By doing it in a way that, when you get done, each of you will be able to say to the other, "Live and be well."

This is not the message you will get from your Greek Chorus. To be sure, they will justify their advice by saying that they are only looking out for your best interests. But to do that, they must first know what your best interests are. Unfortunately, they don't, which is why their advice will get you into so much trouble, despite all their good intentions. It is not in your best interests for things to get out of hand. Nevertheless, that is exactly what will happen if you follow their advice.

Ironically, most divorcing husbands and wives know that their Greek Chorus is, at best, a mixed blessing. Nevertheless, they have a problem. Their Greek Chorus is also their supply line—the means by which they get information and support. That is why they listen. That is why they are so afraid to turn a deaf ear to them.

I am not suggesting that you do not need help. You do. I am only suggesting that turning to your Greek Chorus for that purpose will not help. It will only make things worse. If the two of you do not want to come away with misguided advice and conflicting opinions, you will have to employ the same supply line, not different ones. If you want to get information or to get help that will truly benefit the two of you, then you will have to go off together. It is the only way to avoid being given different answers to the same question.

CHAPTER 13

THE CARPENTER, HIS WIFE, HIS BEST FRIEND AND HIS FATHER

More often than not, the judgments that we make
in other people's lives are wrong when they
are not otherwise irrelevant.
Worse, they are usually of no benefit to anyone
save perhaps ourselves.

I said that if you are not careful, your Greek Chorus will knock at your knees—instead of giving you support, they will undermine your confidence. What can you do to prevent this from happening? Here is how I learned the answer to this.

Many years ago, I worked with a couple who had been married for a number of years and had a six-year-old daughter. The husband was self-employed as a handyman/carpenter. His wife had worked before their marriage, but now stayed home taking care of their daughter.

Since he did not work for a corporate employer, and never would, he was not going to come away with any retirement benefits at the end of the day. Nevertheless, being very industrious, he had a game plan of his own. He and his wife owned their own home. Through hard work, he had managed to save enough money to make a down payment on a second home, that he used as rental property. He did not derive any income from this second home, and that was not its purpose. He used the rent to pay the mortgage and other expenses. His game plan was that, when he retired one day, the mortgages on both of their homes would be satisfied. That second home would now be income producing, and that would be his pension.

While we never discussed this, I got the sense that because he worked as hard as he did, he was not at home as much as his wife (and perhaps he) would have liked. His focus was on his game plan. As a result, he didn't take sufficient notice of what was going on along the way. What was going on was that his wife had become emotionally involved with his best friend, who was probably at their home more than her husband was.

It was a tragedy on all counts. The two of them were very decent, hardworking people. Never once did either of them cast aspersions on the other. Nor did either of them ever do anything out of line. In fact, I was repeatedly amazed by some of the things he said.

The tragedy in this, from his standpoint, was that with one swift blow, he had lost everything he had worked for and dreamed of. He had lost his wife, he would no longer be living with his daughter on a day-to-day basis, and because he and his wife would be splitting everything they had—she retaining the home that they lived in and he the second home—he had lost his game plan as well.

One of the things that so impressed me about him was how hard he tried to make as much sense as he could out of something that didn't make any sense at all. His wife was a very nice person, and he knew that. He certainly did not understand why or how she and his best friend had formed the relationship that they had, but he was smart enough and balanced enough to know that one didn't cancel out the other. Never once did I hear a word of recrimination from him. Despite all that had happened, his wife was still basically a good person.

He was also trying very hard to do what had to be done and to act as responsibly as he could. His problem, however, was his Greek Chorus—in this case his father—who was obviously very angry at his son's wife for what she had done. The message that he repeatedly heard from his father was the familiar one that every one in his position gets—"After what she did to you, you would be willing to do that. Then you must be a fool."

He struggled with this for some time and it was a constant sore point for him. One day he finally found a way to solve his problem. He said something that I will never forget. I only wish that I had been smart enough to think of it myself. What he said was, "You know, the only people who have a right to express an opinion about what is going on in this room are the people sitting in this room." With that he had found a way to close the door on his father.

CHAPTER 14

STORIES

I cannot tell you whether there is life after death,
but I do know that there can be life after divorce.

Each of us go through our lives telling stories to ourselves about ourselves. It is our way of making sense of what happens to us. Moreover, it is essential that we keep our stories straight.

It is not very hard to do that when good things happen to us. For example, you have worked very hard. You have put in a great deal of time and effort. You therefore think it only appropriate that you be made the next vice president in charge of sales. When the time comes, you are promoted and given that job. That will not be difficult to integrate into your ongoing story. That is because it affirms your story—confirms the view that you have of yourself. Put another way, it does not call your story into question.

Now consider the other possibility. You have worked very hard. You have put in a great deal of time and effort. Again, you think it only appropriate that you be promoted and made the next vice president in charge of sales. But they pass you over and select someone else. Now you have a problem. It is going to be very difficult to integrate what has happened to you into your ongoing story. What has happened does not affirm your view of yourself. In fact, it has done a great deal of damage to your story, so much that it may be necessary for you to leave your firm and seek employment elsewhere—with a firm that appreciates you more—for you to keep your story straight.

Except for the death of a child or someone extremely close, divorce is perhaps the most difficult experience that any of us will ever negotiate in our lives. For that very reason, it is also one of the most difficult to integrate into our on-going stories. It does too much damage to it. But then, you don't need me to tell you that.

There is something, however, that you may not be aware of. That is that you are faced with a developmental task. If that seems strange, it is because we normally don't think of adults having to perform developmental tasks. That is only for children. Nevertheless, it is true. In fact, your future well-being is critically dependent on how well you perform it. That task is to integrate what has happened to you in your life—your divorce—into your ongoing story. It is to see to it that it does the least possible damage to your story. It is to make enough sense of it that it does not cripple you, as it does so many divorcing husbands and wives.

Admittedly, that is not going to be easy. It is to ask you to try to make sense of something that, on a fundamental level, doesn't make any sense at all. That is always the case with tragedies. And what is happening to you is a tragedy.

Nor is this something that anyone can do for you. The most they can do is point you in the right direction. The most they can do is tell you what not to do—what will only make things worse than they already are. All they can do is tell you what will only make it more difficult for you to perform that development task.

With that in mind, I would like to remind you of something you already know, and that is that a physician has no power to heal you. You cut yourself and go to a physician for him to attend you. He cleans out the wound. He applies some medication. He puts a protective covering on it. He then sends you home and tells you not to pick at your wound. What else does he do? Nothing. Rather, he relies on the fact that there is a natural healing process, and that if he has removed all of the impurities and if you do not pick at your wound and impede it, it will proceed on its own.

The same is true of your divorce and the developmental task that you are faced with. There is a natural healing process in life. To be sure, it will take time, but time will eventually do what words (all your answers and explanations) are incapable of doing. In fact, if you are not careful, the words that so many people fill your head with will only interfere with that process. If you are not careful, life's natural healing process will never be allowed to proceed.

What are the impurities here that will impede that natural healing process? They are the hurt and anger, and sometimes the sense of betrayal, which are the natural by-products of your divorce. Unfortunately, those feelings are also the defensive shield that you have thrown up to protect yourself. If things that happen to us in our lives do not make sense, if they threaten our ability to keep our stories straight, all that we can do is react in some way. You cannot deny the reality of what has happened to you. You tried that, but it has not worked. You do not know how to take up arms against it. Nor are you able to cause it to disappear. All that you can do is throw up a protective shield of feelings that will act as a buffer against its damaging effects. To be sure, those feelings will not change anything. But they will at least enable you to do something—to react against what has happened to you rather than to do nothing.

Unfortunately, while those feelings may be your defense, they will invariably get in your way. If you are not careful, they can become your worst enemy. That is because they are infecting your wound. That is because they will impede the natural healing process that you must allow to take place. That is because they will block your efforts to complete the developmental task with which you are faced.

I said that I wrote this book in part because I wanted to offer people going through this difficult experience hope and reason to have hope. I have navigated through these waters for most of my professional life. I want to tell you that my experience is that there can be life after divorce. That is not to make light of what has happened to you or what you are going through. Nor is it to say that I can guarantee that you will find your way to the light at the end of the road. Unfortunately, nothing in life is guaranteed. But it is to insist that you can dramatically affect what will happen. It is to say that you have a choice.

Will you hold onto your hurt and anger and carry it forward with you as a weight on your shoulders? Then there is little hope. The weight of that baggage will be too great. It will be like a dead weight, and will inevitably defeat all of your efforts. Will you somehow find a way to come to terms with what has happened to you—integrate it into your ongoing story—and let go of your hurt and anger? Then there is a real possibility.

There is a moral in this. You must not do anything that will further exacerbate those feelings. Nor can you give them free rein. That is simply a luxury you cannot afford. Rather, you must do everything that you can to hold them in check.

Perhaps you can also better understand what I meant when I said earlier that you still need one another—that it is important that, when you are through, each of you is able to say to the other "Live and be well." It has to do with the stories that each of you must necessarily tell yourself about yourself. You may be going your own separate ways. Nevertheless, it will still make it easier for you to keep your story straight if your husband or wife is able to say that and, on some level at least, mean it. It will make it easier for him or her if you are able to say it as well.

CHAPTER 15

POISONING YOUR OWN WELL

All too often we become our own worst enemy
rather than our own best friend.

It is sad but true that most divorcing husbands and wives make it more difficult for themselves. How do they do that? By telling themselves the wrong stories. By telling themselves stories that invariably end, "I was stupid," or "I was just a fool."

I remember a couple with whom I worked a number of years ago where the wife did just this. She and her husband had been married for a very long time and had three children, two of whom were already grown and a younger child who was just finishing high school. It had been her decision to get a divorce, and I knew that it had been a painful one. After she and her husband had signed their agreement, and while she was collecting her things after he had left, I said I knew this had been a difficult decision for her and that I wished her well. She thanked me but then surprised me by saying, "I let him take advantage of me for years. He was just too strong for me."

Why was I so surprised? First, because she was doing a lot of damage to her story. Second, because what she was telling herself wasn't even true.

To be sure, we are each free to organize our experience in any number of ways. In the context here, she could have placed the blame on herself or she could have assigned it to her husband. She could also have said that there was really no one to blame—that this is just what had happened. She took the first tack. She joined forces with the prosecuting attorney. Despite the fact that the evidence really didn't point in only one direction—that the fault really was hers—she accepted the indictment that she was guilty as charged.

Ironically, the story this woman was telling herself wasn't even true. I know that she had convinced herself that it was. For all I know, her Greek Chorus of well-wishers, meaning to be helpful, had implied the same thing when they told her that it was about time that she stopped letting her husband take unfair advantage of her—stopped being his doormat. But that is not really what had happened in her marriage, though even she was convinced of it by now.

What had happened, and what had made her marriage as painfully difficult as it had been, was that she had been given an impossible choice. To be sure, she couldn't change her husband. He was who he was, and nothing was going to change him. Nevertheless she could have left him. But that was not a very attractive option. That would have meant throwing over the entire structure of her life, and that of her children, including the financial security that came with being married to her husband. It is not difficult to understand how she might have had serious second thoughts about doing that.

But her other option was no better. Again, she couldn't change her husband, which meant that if she stayed with him she had to stay with him as he was. That obviously caused very serious problems for her, because who he was ran interference with who she was. To stay with him therefore meant paying the price of having some very important needs of her own left unmet and, worse, certain of her sensibilities trampled upon. Her decision might have been a little easier had she been required to suffer all her husband's indignities in one fell swoop. But that is not how they were meted out. Rather, they came one at a time, and as hard as they were to suffer, it was still easier for her to swallow them, at least one at a time, than to throw over her marriage.

Nor, ironically, was her husband as strong, or she as weak, as she suggested. I know, because I had worked with both of them.

In fact, if someone had asked me to characterize him, I would never have called him strong. Rigid is the word that would have come to mind. Nor would I have ever characterized her as being weak. That wasn't her problem. Her problem was that his rigidity left her no room to maneuver. Or, to put it more accurately, there was no way that she could work with him on his terms without violating her own sense of herself. That was her problem. It was important for her, as it is for most people, to stay in character. In other words, she didn't want to become someone other than who she was just to make peace with him. But there was no way to make peace with him other than on his terms, since he was not going to change and meet her half way.

Finally, the story that she was telling herself didn't explain why she eventually decided to separate from him. Certainly he had not gotten any weaker or she any stronger. They were the same people today that they were yesterday. What had changed were her circumstances. Her children were older. She was now more financially secure in leaving him than she would have been years before. Most important, the little indignities had begun to add up, and had taken their toll. If she finally left, it was simply because she was no longer able to stay.

Why am I telling you this? Because far too many separating and divorcing husbands and wives do exactly what this woman did to herself. They poison their own well. They tell themselves stories that impose self-inflicting wounds. They become their own worst enemies rather than their own best friends.

CHAPTER 16

QUESTIONS

If you want a better answer, you will have to ask a better question.

We are brought up to succeed, not to fail. If there is a job to do, we are supposed to do it. If there is a problem to solve, we are supposed to solve it. If there is an obstacle to overcome, we are supposed to overcome it. If there is a question to answer, we are supposed answer it.

As a general rule, this makes good sense. Nevertheless, that is not always the case. As we go through our lives, there are times when we find ourselves confronted with questions to which there are no answers, or at least no adequate ones. In those instances, the better part of wisdom is to let go of them. Admittedly, it is hard for us to accept this—that there are questions that have no answers. That is like saying there is a crime but no criminal. After all, someone must have done it. Nevertheless, it is true.

What does this have to do with your divorce? A great deal. We do not ask questions out of idle curiosity. We ask them for reasons. We ask them to make sense of what has happened to us in our lives—in this case, in our marriage. The problem is that what has happened really doesn't make very much sense to us, or at least very much sense that we are able to see.

To be sure, you have given yourself answers. But those answers have not helped. They have not relieved your pain or your sense of loss. They have not assuaged your feeling that you have been wronged. If anything, they have only made things worse. That is because the answers you have given yourself tell you that you have been made to suffer a great injustice and are the innocent victim of a terrible crime.

Unfortunately, it is not possible for you to understand what has happened to you, let alone make sense of it. That is because it is not possible for you to see your own role in what has happened. I did not say fault. I did not say complicity. I just said role. Of necessity, you cannot help but feel that you are where you are because of what someone else has done or been unwilling to do. Put simply, you cannot help but see yourself as being the innocent victim in all of this. And since you did not get married to get divorced—since this is not where you expected or intended to be or where you feel you deserve to be—you are understandably overwhelmed by feelings of hurt and anger, and perhaps even more.

It is not possible for you to see it differently. The way that you have organized the experience of your marriage, and now divorce, leads to one and only one possible conclusion. That is because implicit in every question is its answer. If you see what happened to you as a crime—and it will be difficult for you to see it any other way—then there must be someone who committed that crime. There must be someone at fault.

I am not going to tell you that you are wrong. Since I have not led your life, it would be very inappropriate for me to make judgements in it. I am not even going to try to change how you think. You wouldn't listen to me anyway. You certainly won't thank me. That is because you are deeply invested in the answers you have given yourself, which is why you cling to them, and rehearse them, over and over.

What I am going to suggest, therefore, is not that you change your answers, but that you let go of your question. Your answers haven't helped you make any sense of what has happened to you. Like all crimes, and even more so of tragedies, what has happened doesn't make any sense. That is why we are left with such painful feelings. To be sure, there are reasons why we hold onto those feelings, as painful as they are. That is because, at times, feeling something, even pain, is preferable to feeling nothing.

What are you to do? Psychologists have an expression that may help you. You do not solve your problems in therapy. If therapy is successful, they simply go away. In other words, you have a problem in the first place only because of the way in which you have organized your experience.

What that means here is that you have been left with a problem because the questions you are asking leave you no way out. They lead to a dead end. They are premised on the assumption that you are the innocent victim of a terrible crime. Obviously, you cannot accept that in silence. But you are helpless to do anything about it. That is your dilemma. As I said, you cannot possibly solve it. That is why the better counsel is to organize your experience in such a way that it will go away.

How can you do that? I will not pretend that it will be easy. But I will give you a start. Remember, if you want a better answer, you will have to ask a better question. Of necessity, the question that you have been asking—how did such a terrible thing happen to me?—forces you to look back. However, there is no future in the past. All that is there are your failed hopes and expectations, and with it the disappointment, the hurt, and possibly the sense of betrayal, that are the inevitable by-products of what has happened to you in your marriage. What you must do, therefore, is find a way to look forward. To do that, you will first have to ask yourself a better question. Ask, "Do my feelings of hurt and anger change anything? Are they harming me more than anyone else? Are they making it more difficult or less difficult for me to get on with my life? Are they allowing me to heal or are they just poisoning my wound?"

It will not be possible for you to ask those questions, however, if you continue to ask the ones that you have been asking. It is not possible to go backward and go forward at the same time. All you will do is pull yourself apart. You will therefore have to choose.

CHAPTER 17

STAYING IN CHARACTER

If you do the wrong thing for the right reason, the only thing you know for sure is that you did the wrong thing.

I said earlier that each of us goes through our lives telling stories to ourselves about ourselves. I must now add something. Each of us has a role that we play in that story. We may not be conscious of that role. We might not even be able to describe it. But we play that part nevertheless. To be sure, it may not be exactly who we were when the play (story) began. But it is the role that we have adopted and grown into along the way. Moreover, it is a part that we have studied carefully for some time. It is who we have chosen to be and, therefore, who we are.

Under normal circumstances, it is not difficult for any of us to stay in character. That is because our part does not test us. We have rehearsed it so well and played it for so long that we can perform it almost by rote. It is very different, however, when we get to a more difficult place, or where, as here, the plot takes an unexpected turn. Then it will take far more effort to stay in character.

The scene that is unfolding is a case in point. What is happening to you will not show you off to good advantage. No one of us is at his or her best at times like this. Others may even have to excuse your behavior if you depart somewhat from the script from time to time. If you do, it is because the story line was not of your own making. It is because it will test you to the limit. Nevertheless, it is critically important that you stay in character. To depart from that role is to become someone other than who you are.

Under normal circumstances, it would not be necessary to remind someone of this. Most people know this, even if they do not give much thought to it. Over the years, they have crafted who it is that they are, and when they look at themselves in the mirror they like the picture they see. More important, what they see doesn't make great demands of them. Nor does it force them to ask difficult questions.

It is very different, however, when things take a sudden turn for the worse. It is particularly difficult if our whole world has become upended. Then there will be no end of questions that we will be forced to ask. Worse, there will not seem to be any answers, or at least any adequate ones. It is then, more than ever, that it behooves us to try to stay in character. At times such as this, our role—who we like to believe we are—may be the only solid thing that we have to hold onto.

There will be something else that will make it more difficult for you to stay in character. That is your husband's or wife's performance. Inevitably, they will have a very different view of the drama that is unfolding. They will also have a very different opinion as to their own part in it. Thus, while you may see them as being the villain in the piece, they will undoubtedly see themselves as being the innocent victim. In fact, in the story that they tell themselves about themselves and what has happened in their lives, they may assign the role of the villain to you.

This will inevitably cause problems. If the two of you are playing different roles in different stories, that is only going to make it that much more difficult for you to keep your story straight. Given the role that you have assigned to yourself, it will not be possible for you to understand, let alone find any adequate justification for, how your husband or wife is acting. If you are the innocent victim in all of this, as you cannot help but feel that you are, then their conduct will necessarily appear to be that much more inappropriate. That is going to leave you with a problem.

Should you stay in character or should you respond in kind? My advice is that you stay in character.

Am I suggesting that you turn the other cheek? No. If you feel that you have no choice but to take a certain course of action, then you will have to take it. All that I am saying is that you must think carefully before you act. You must also ask yourself what will be the consequences of your actions. And if it is not clear what those consequences will be—and it is never possible to anticipate all of the unintended consequences of our actions—you must think again.

You must remember something else. No matter how clear it may seem to you, it is simply not possible for you to see accurately what is happening. You are far too close to what is going on to be able to do that. You are also only seeing a small part of it. Worse, you are looking at it through a lens of painful feelings that not only distorts what you are able to see but also exaggerates certain aspects of it. To be sure, you will have very strong convictions in terms of what you think you see. Nevertheless, the strength of your convictions is no guarantee of their accuracy.

What are you to do? I have suggested one thing, namely that your best bet is to stay in character, since that is the one thing that you know for sure. I will suggest another. It is something that you should always keep in mind whenever you are considering a certain course of action. If you do the wrong thing for the right reason, the only thing that you know for sure is that you did the wrong thing.

I want to pose one last question. Let us assume that you follow my advice and do everything that you can to stay in character. Does that mean that your husband or wife will as well? Put another way, isn't it possible that you will run a risk if you do?

Of course there is a risk. It is never possible to know for sure what the consequences of our actions will be. Will they be reciprocated in kind? Will they have no effect at all? Will they inure to our disadvantage? Obviously, those are all possibilities. Nor am I suggesting otherwise.

But the same is true if you step out of character. There is necessarily a risk in that as well. Thus, the appropriate question to ask yourself is which course of conduct provides you with the better assurance and the least risk? In the imperfect world that we live in, it is not possible to eliminate risk. There are risks in whatever you do. All you can do is choose between them.

I can tell you from my experience that there is no question which of those risks is better. To be sure, if your husband or wife plays by the rule that "there are no rules" and "anything goes," he or she will make things more difficult for you. But, ironically, that does not mean that it will benefit them. Nor, in most instances, will it really prejudice you. That is because most of the inappropriate conduct that divorcing husbands and wives engage in has little, if any, effect on how things will ultimately turn out in the end. It just makes a terrible mess of things along the way.

The truth is that if your husband (or wife) is intent on going down in flames in order to have it his way, there is really little that you will be able to do to stop him. To be sure, there will be those who will tell you otherwise. What they will neglect to tell you is that those things are almost always after the fact. They are like cleaning up the *Exxon Valdez* oil spill after the damage has already been done. What they will fail to tell you is that you would be better served devoting your efforts to avoiding the *Valdez* oil spill rather than in devising ways to clean it up. To be sure, it may come to that. But it still makes more sense to try to prevent it.

There is something else that you have not been told. It is important that you know it. If your husband (or wife) decides to play that game, there is only way to beat him. That is to play the same game—to become just like him.

Needless to say, you do not want to do that. That was never your role. Nor can you afford to. When all is said and done and your divorce is finally concluded, it will be necessary for you to go back and attend to your story—set it straight. If you allow yourself to step too far out of character, it will only make it that much more difficult for you to do that.

I want to give you one last good reason to stay in character, particularly if you have children. There are other people in your lives who also have stories that they must tell themselves—stories that they must keep straight. Moreover, since their stories are inextricably bound up in yours, they are understandably looking to you. In fact, they will be looking to you now more than ever. Thus, to damage your story is to damage their story as well. Obviously, you do not want to do that. They are having a difficult enough time as it is.

CHAPTER 18

TELLING THE CHILDREN: WHEN, HOW AND WHAT

God gave us children to make up for everything else that he also gave to us.

It is said that children develop emotionally based on the strength of the bond between their parents. If that is so, then they will be affected when that bond is broken by their parents' separation and divorce. Nevertheless, the lasting damage that is done to children is not occasioned by the fact of their parents' separation. It is occasioned, first, by how their parents go about their divorce—whether they went down the right road or the wrong road—and, second, by the relationship that their parents are able to maintain, at least when it comes to them, following their separation.

Divorcing husbands and wives sometimes make the mistake of thinking that their children will be affected only if they become involved in contested custody litigation. That is not so. Children are affected by whatever contentious disagreements their parents have, whether it affects them directly or not. That is because it weakens the bond they depend on. That is because they get drawn into the middle of it anyway. That is why it is so important that you do not go down the wrong road. If you do, you will take your children with you.

Even if you avoid that, this will still leave you with a number of questions. You will also inevitably encounter problems along the way as your children attempt to adjust and adapt to what is taking place in your and their lives. I am not going to attempt to address all those problems here. If the need arises, there are qualified people who you can turn to for help. All that you need do now is agree you will seek their help should the need arise, and that you will turn to them together. Remember, it is going off on your own that will create the problem and cause things to get out of hand.

Nevertheless, I do want to address one or two questions that you will inevitably have. When do you tell your children that you are planning to separate (and divorce)? What do you tell them about that decision? How do you tell them? Since telling your children (even if they already know, as older children often do) will be one of the hardest things that you will ever have to do, it is important that you give thought to these questions before you rush on ahead.

Let me start with the last question. The answer is simple. It is also extremely important. You must tell them everything of importance together.

Telling them together serves a number of purposes. The first is that it reassures them. By definition, what you are telling them is that the two of you are separating—that you are each going your own separate way. Obviously, that is very threatening to them. That is why it is important, at the same time, to reinforce the fact that you will still be in this together, at least for them. But, since words are not as significant for children as actions, it is not enough for you to say this. They must also see it. They will not see it, however, if each of you tells it to them separately. That will only reinforce their anxiety.

Your children will realize that their world is changing, that the two of you are no longer one, and that you will each be going off in separate directions. While that may meet your needs, it does not meet theirs. On the contrary, it will undermine the very structure of their lives. Thus, while you may no longer need or want one another, they want and very much need both of you.

There is something that they need even more, and that is the feeling that both of you need and want them. Ironically, that is important even where, because they have already been drawn into your conflict, they have taken sides. More often than not, they have done that only to protect themselves, and because they felt that their best interests were better served by being the ally of one of you rather than the other. Sometimes it is because they blame you for what has happened. It is irrelevant. That still does not mean that they do not need you even if, as is sometimes the case, they feel the need to distance themselves from you presently.

Being told things by each of you separately will only tend to reinforce all of these problems. This can be true of unimportant things as well as important things. First, they do not know what is important or unimportant. They certainly do not know what to do with the information you give them. Is it something that, if one of you tells them, they should not tell the other? They will tend to assume that. Even if that is not the case, how are they to determine that? Second, hearing things from the two of you separately only underscores the division between you. To be sure, it may seem innocent enough to you. But from their standpoint (and that is the only one that counts) it will appear as if the two of you are in separate armed camps. This is particularly true if what either of you tells them comes laden with negativity about the other. And it will come with negativity even if you are not aware of it. If you feel negative about your husband or wife, how can you not convey that?

Finally, what you tell them separately will tend to undermine their security. They do not want to be in the middle. Nor do they want to be disloyal to either of you. Certainly they do not want to have to choose between you. But that is where they will be left if you talk to them separately. One of you is not there.

Telling them the important things that you have to say together, with both of you present, avoids most of these problems. It certainly minimizes them. Your children do not have to worry whether listening to what you are telling them means choosing sides or being disloyal. How could it when they are hearing it from the two of you, or from one of you with the other present? Nor do they have to worry whether it must be kept secret. You have told it in such a way that it is not a secret to begin with. More importantly, you have given them permission to be loyal to both of you and to accept love from one of you without feeling disloyal to the other.

What do you tell your children? Here what you do not say is as important as what you do say. Though it should be obvious, I will say it anyway. Do not get into history—the history of how the two of you got to this point in your lives. They will not be able to understand it. If one or both of you does not really understand it, how can you expect them to understand it? Nor is it possible to say it without recrimination. Besides, they do not need or want to know all the *whys* and *wherefores*. They are irrelevant. It is history, and it should be left as that. In short, the only thing you should tell them or that they need to know is that the two of you have had problems you have been unable to resolve, although you have tried, and that you have therefore decided that it would be best if you separated (and divorced).

The second thing that you must not do is place blame. For one of you, this will be about the hardest thing you will have to do—to share the blame, so to speak, with your husband or wife who wants the divorce, perhaps over your strong objection. You will want your children to know whose fault it really is—at least as you see it. You may have an equally strong need for them not to blame you for what has happened to them, and to let them know the truth. It is therefore going to be extremely difficult for one of you to tell them that this was a joint decision the two of you came to, let alone a necessity. In fact, everything within you will cry out against it. You may even defend yourself here by saying that you do not want to lie to them. And from your standpoint, at least, it will be a lie.

Unfortunately, that is not the issue. The question you must ask yourself is not whether what they are hearing is a lie. The question is, "For whose benefit am I telling them the truth, theirs or mine?" Your children have no need or desire to know the truth. They will not even understand it. Again, if you really don't understand how your marriage has gotten to this point, how possibly can they? Nor will it be of any benefit to them. On the contrary, it will only put them where they do not want to be and do not deserve to be—in the middle.

If it is really your children and not yourself who you are trying to protect, you must not give in to that need, no matter how strong it is, and no matter how understandable. In fact, when all is said and done, it will be the test of whose interests you are putting first. Telling your children the truth may help you keep your story straight. But it will only make it that much more difficult for them to keep their story straight. You must therefore find a way to keep your story straight without messing up their story at the same time. Perhaps that means letting your husband or wife do the talking, and you standing by silently. Perhaps it means telling them a white lie. There are good reasons not to lie. Nevertheless, as the term "white lie" indicates, as a general rule it is only wrong to lie when you are lying to protect yourself rather than someone else. Telling the truth to accomplish the same end is no better.

This raises the next question. Should you tell each of your children separately or all together? That is a hard question; it will depend on the circumstances. All things being equal, it would be better to tell them all together. While, on the one hand, there is something to be said for a one-on-one discussion, it might also increase their anxiety. While they might each want to be alone with the two of you, there is comfort in numbers. There can be individual time later with the two of you and just one of them. The one thing that you do not want is for them learn about it by rumor. Thus, if you decide to speak with them separately—and as a general rule it should be the eldest first, down the line—it should be proximate in time to avoid that possibility.

When do you tell your children? Just as there is never a good time to get divorced, there is never a good time to tell your children that you are getting divorced. It is just before Christmas, just before one of their birthdays, or just before or after they leave or return from their summer vacation. Again, the question is not when is the right time. It is when is the wrong time. Telling them just before they are to leave on vacation and be without one or both of you for any period of time is obviously not the right time.

Another critical question is when you will tell them in terms of the actual separation itself. A day before? Six months before? The answer here is a lot simpler. They are going to need some time to adjust to the shock of your separation. That will be easier if the one who is leaving your home is there for a period of time to help ease that shock rather than immediately leave and only add to it. Thus, a day before is the wrong time.

Nor, however, do you want to announce your decision six months before. Remember, children's sense of time is different from yours. If six months will seem like a very long time to you, it can seem like an eternity to them. Remember also that they put more significance in actions than words. If you say that you are separating but they still see you living under the same roof six months later, what are they to believe? Finally, remember that they may be hoping against hope that you will change your mind. Six months is therefore far too long. It violates all of these considerations. What is the right time? Ideally, about two or three weeks.

There is one other factor that will, and should, affect your timing. That is where the two of you are in the process. Remember, you are not just stating an historical fact—that the two of you are separating (and divorcing). More importantly, you want to assure them that the two of you have made appropriate arrangements for them, and all will be well. I am not saying that it is not at times necessary and appropriate, at least with older children, to also be realistic with them. But it serves no useful purpose to burden them with problems that they may not fully understand, cannot emotionally handle, and have little or no ability to deal with.

It is not possible to do this, however, when the two of you have not sat down and decided these things yourselves, and therefore do not know exactly what is going to happen. Ideally, then, it would be far better to announce your decision when you are in a position to assure them that all of the necessary arrangements have been made and (at least as far as where they will live and with whom) what they are, that there is no need for them to worry, and that the two of you are going to take care of them in the future, just as you have in the past. It will be a lot easier for the two of you (or at least for one of you) to do that when you are able to see that yourself. But you will not be able to see that until the two of you have worked out all these arrangements, at least in broad outline.

Sometimes events get ahead of themselves, however. For example, there are times when it makes good sense to physically separate even though all of the "i's" have not been dotted or the "t's" crossed. There are other times when you have no real choice. Since it had never been your intention to get into all of the nitty gritty with them anyway—who will be responsible for the payment of their after school activities and their un-reimbursed medical expenses—it is not necessary to have ironed out all of these details before you sit down with them. If at all possible, the basics should be in place and you should be in a position to tell them with whom they will be living and where—in their present home or somewhere else.

There is something else that you can do to reinforce the continuity in their lives, despite the reality of your separation. Particularly if they are old enough (and they do not have to be very old), involve them in the move that the one who is leaving the home is making (if that is the case). In other words, instead of just introducing them to his or her new apartment or other living accommodations, let them have some involvement in it beforehand. It would also help if the parent who is remaining in the marital residence (if that is the case) shows some interest in the other's new living accommodations and accompanies him or her and the children when they first go to see it. All of this helps to soften the breach. The more they are able to see you work together, even in little things, the easier it is for them. It also tends to reinforce the fact that you are both still there for them.

Admittedly, I have just touched the surface here. Since I do not know the particulars of your life, that is all that I could do. Undoubtedly, there will be other questions that will arise along the way. How will you handle them? There is only one decision that you have to make. Should they arise, you will deal with them (and, if need be, seek help) together.

PART III

Finding Your Way—Avoiding the Hazards

CHAPTER 19

SEEING WHAT YOU ARE SUPPOSED TO SEE

The mythology is that you turn to lawyers because lawyers will protect you.
The truth is that, having turned to lawyers, you will now need protection.

Like you, those who seek my help come to me with a picture of their divorce already sketched in their minds. Unfortunately, it is the wrong picture. It is going to get them into trouble. That is because it is the picture that has been painted by our adversarial legal system. As such, it incorporates all the assumptions that support and lend credence to adversarial divorce proceedings.

Their picture does something else. As with Hans Christian Anderson's story, *The Emperor's New Clothes*, it persuades them to see what they are supposed to see. It leads them to believe that running off to lawyers for help is a perfectly natural thing to do. It isn't. It is very unnatural.

Enabling husbands and wives who come to me to see what they are not supposed to see is never easy. I have to work very hard at it. I use two means for that purpose. The first is sayings. The second is what I refer to as silly little stories that are not so silly. The purpose of the sayings is to underscore some simple truths. In most instances they are nothing more than common sense. Nevertheless, the picture that they come to me with disables them from being able to see these truths. An example is one that

I have already told you, namely, that if you do not take control of the events in your life the events in your life will take control of you.

The purpose of my silly little stories, which are really parodies, is a little different. It is to get the two of them to see that, ironically, it is the stories that they are telling themselves, derived from their pre-programmed picture of the world of divorce, that are really rather silly.

I am going to tell you one such story. It is one I commonly tell couples when I meet with them for the first time. In this case, the husband and wife I am meeting with have been married for ten years. They have two small children, ages six and four. The three of us are sitting at a round table in a small conference room in my office. Along two of the walls in the room are floor-to-ceiling book cases filled with law books. To the side of me is a small stand with a telephone on it. Turning to the two of them, I say:

"I know this is going to surprise you, but I have been sitting here night after night for the last ten years waiting for the two of you to call me. Not that I knew you would be getting a divorce. How could I have possibly known that? But knowing that I had gone to law school and had a license to practice law, it would never have occurred to me that the two of you would make any of the important decisions in your lives without first getting my opinion and advice. And I must tell you that it has been very lonely and very ego deflating to sit here night after night waiting for the two of you to call me, while you just went about the business of your lives without first seeking my advice. You certainly didn't call me when you were planning to get married, though I was sitting here by the telephone then, too, and had some very good advice for you. No, you just took it upon yourselves to make all of the important decisions in your lives on your own—where you would get married, who you would invite, what you would serve, and where you would go on your honeymoon—without first getting my good opinion. But I must tell you that it always surprises me how, when people decide to change the direction in their lives—to divorce rather than marry—just how smart I become. Suddenly the telephone rings off the hook. Now, no one would consider taking a step without first getting my opinion.

"And I want to congratulate you. I don't know what took you so long to get here. But I did go to law school and I do have a license to practice law. More important, unlike the two of you, I have read all the decisions in the books in this room indicating what the law considers to be in the best interest of your children. I have written on the subject. I have lectured about it. In fact, I am considered to be somewhat of an authority when it comes to what the law considers to be in the best interest of children. That being the case, since I have to assume that you only want what is best for your children, and since I am clearly the only expert in the room when it comes to what the law considers to be in their best interest, I think that you should make the first decision when it comes to your children's future well-being. That is, from this point forward, I will make all of the important decisions in their lives.

"If I were to say anything that silly, if you had any sense, you would get up and get out of here as fast as you can. You are obviously talking to a madman—someone who believes that because he went to law school and has a license to practice law, he knows better than you what is best for your children. You will excuse me. You get it when it comes to your children, but you lose it when it comes to your money. Maybe because I went to law school and have a license to practice law, I know better than you do what is best for your money. I hate to disappoint you. I didn't raise your children. I didn't make your money. I am not an expert when it comes to either.

"But wait a moment. What about all the law books in this room and all of the decisions in them indicating what the law considers to be in the best interest of your children? Aren't they important? I didn't say that. They are very important. But they do not contain your legal rights, as you have been led to believe. They contain your legal penalties. In other words, if the two of you are not smart enough and responsible enough to sit down and decide what is going to happen to your children, lawyers like myself will be glad to pull out our law books, put them on the table, and make those decisions for you. And we will do the same when it comes to your money."

What is the moral of this story? It is to remind you that, until this point, you were the ones who made all of the important decisions in your lives. As I express it, you were the captains of your ship, you had your hands firmly on the wheel, and you were perfectly capable of charting the course of your lives. I do not know whether all of the decisions you made in the past were good ones. Maybe some of them were and some of them weren't. The one thing I know is that it would never have occurred to you to let anyone else make those decisions for you.

Unfortunately, all of that changes once the prospect of divorce looms on the horizon. It is as if the sky has suddenly gotten very dark, the wind has begun to howl and the sea has begun to swell. To be sure, your hands are still firmly on the wheel, but they are frozen. Worse, wherever you look there are beacons of light beckoning to you. "Over here." "No, over here." As a result, you are paralyzed with fear and do not know in which direction to turn.

It is this that so overwhelms divorcing husbands and wives and causes them to go off on their own and resort to self-help. It is this that causes them to buy into legal mythology—the idea that they have a legal problem—and run off to lawyers.

But don't you have a legal problem now that you have decided to divorce? Of course not. You have a personal problem that simply has certain legal implications. (Again, you know that when it comes to your children.) The same was true of your marriage, however. Marrying someone has certain legal implications. You had to get a license. You assumed certain legal obligations. But that didn't mean that you turned to lawyers when you got married. And you certainly did not allow them to make the important decisions for you. Nor is there any law that says that you have to do that now.

This raises a question. Would a divorce lawyer suggest that you made a mistake in the past when you made all of the important decisions in your lives on your own, without getting his opinion? Of course not. In fact, he would acknowledge that it was perfectly appropriate for your to have done that. But if that was true before, why is it not true now?

If pressed, what a lawyer would say is that it was appropriate in the past because you were out in the calm sea, the sun was shining, and the wind was gently blowing. All of that has suddenly changed, however. Having decided to divorce, you now find yourselves in unchartered legal waters and since you are not skilled legal navigators, you are bound to lose your way. Worse, if you are not careful, you will be eaten by all of the legal sharks lurking in those waters.

Again, this is simply legal nonsense. Worse, it is very dangerous nonsense. You are not in unchartered legal waters. You are just in unfamiliar waters. That is why you are so frightened and so overwhelmed. But there is a safe harbor out there. You will not reach it, however, if you allow your fear to get the better of you or your feelings to overwhelm you. Nor will you reach it if you allow the blazing light of the abstractions that divorce lawyers forever invoke blind you to where you must get.

What will happen if you buy into the legal mythology that your problem is that you have wandered into unchartered legal waters? The first thing that will happen is that you will disenfranchise yourselves. You used to be the ones who appropriately made the important decisions in your life. But that was before, when you were out in the calm sea. (If the truth be told, it was not always so calm. Most married couples have had to weather storms in their lives in the past.) However, if you really are in unchartered legal waters, since neither of you has gone to law school and studied divorce law, then you are not qualified to navigate through these waters. Only divorce lawyers are. What that means in simple terms is that if you buy into legal mythology, you are going to give lawyers license to approach the bridge, push you both aside, and take over your ship.

But don't the two of you need help? Of course you do. Not the help of those who are going to take over your lives, however, offering no better excuse than that they went to law school. Rather, the help of someone who has been through these waters many times before and is familiar with them—someone who can guide you to that safe harbor. Again, not by taking over your ship and making all of the important decisions in your lives. Rather, by standing next to you, talking to you in reassuring terms, and helping you regain your confidence so that the two of you can make those decisions yourselves.

It is your ship. Don't ever surrender it to someone else.

CHAPTER 20

FEAR

Lawyers do not know what is best for us.
Nor are they necessarily wise.
They are just people who went to law school.

Those who come to me know that I am a lawyer. In fact, they no doubt take some comfort in that. Nevertheless, I always tell them that the best they are going to get from me is not anything that I learned in law school or read in a law book. What they are going to get from me is my experience.

To be sure, the two of them undoubtedly view themselves as having a legal problem. Why else would they be consulting with a lawyer? But that is not how I view them or their problem. To me, they are two people who have suddenly and unexpectedly found themselves confronted with a very difficult and overwhelming practical problem. In its simplest terms, that problem is how each of them is going to be able to manage financially in the future, and the obligation that one of them, based on the circumstances of their marriage, should have to the other to be concerned with how he or she will be able to do that. If they have children, this includes their needs as well. Most important, it includes the question of how each of them is going to be able to be the important influence in their children's lives in the future that they have been in the past, and how they and their children are going to be able to enjoy one another's company and companionship.

I refer to this problem as an immense forest they must

somehow get through, and then over the mountain, hopefully to the clearing on the other side. Invariably, they are very frightened by the prospect before them. That is because they have never been through this territory before. Besides, no one wants to go through a forest alone, particularly at night. Understandably, they would like to have the hand of someone who has been through it many times before, and who can hopefully get them safely to the other side.

That is what I do. That is my role. I tell them that I view myself as a guide. I have been through this territory more times than I can count, and have helped countless couples, just like the two of them, get through it safely. To be sure, I believe that they should make the important decisions in their lives now, just as they always have in the past. But I do have a lot of experience here that they do not have, and I would like them to have the benefit of it.

I also want to help assuage their fears, for their fears are one of the things that will cause them to take their eyes off the mark. Understandably, they are frightened. But that does not mean that they should allow those fears to get so out of hand that they feel impelled to turn over the decisions in their lives to others, which is what they will do if they go down the wrong road. After all, what qualifies someone else to make the important decisions in their lives. Certainly not the fact that he or she went to law school and has a license to practice law. Rather, they are still the ones who should make those decisions, for the simple reason that they are the ones who will have to live with them. But this is unfamiliar territory. That is why they will need my help now when they have never needed it before.

Let me now return to my initial inquiry. Why would you and your husband or wife have difficulty doing now what you have always done in the past, namely, make all of the important decisions in your lives? With minor exception, the problems that the two of you must address do not require any special expertise. After all, we are not talking about the federal deficit or global warming. We are talking about your mortgage payments and the price of a new pair of shoes. You have never had difficulty dealing with those issues before. Why would you have such difficulty now?

What I have learned over a lifetime working with divorcing couples who have found themselves faced with these questions is that there are two things. The first is fear. The second is the difficult feelings that each of them find themselves struggling with.

I want to address the first of these, namely, fear. To be more accurate, there are four somewhat different fears. I will start with a simple one. In the past, all the two of you had to do was take one day at a time. When you got married, you were not required to sit down and decide your entire life—where you would live first, whether you would rent or buy, how long you would live there, where you would go after that; how many children you would have, when you would have the first, what the spacing between them would be and when you would stop, and so forth. All that you were required to do was take one day at a time, and there are few of us who have difficulty doing that.

Now, however, it seems as if you must sit down, put your whole life on the table, and decide everything all at once and forever. To make matters worse, there is no going back. In the past, if the two of you made a decision over coffee at breakfast, in most instances you could revisit it, and change your mind, over dinner. Now you will be signing off—putting your name to an agreement—and there will be no going back. Understandably, that is a little frightening.

The second fear is related to the first. You have never done this before. In fact, it is all very new to you. Suppose you forget something? Suppose there is something very important that belongs in your agreement that isn't there? Suppose, suppose?

The third fear is related to the first two. In the past, the two of you were in this together. Whatever problems there were, you had someone by your side. Now you will be going off on your own, or at least that is how it seems. Understandably, that too is frightening.

The last fear, however, is the most overwhelming. That is

the fear that you may not have enough. Most couples barely had enough when they were married. Their credit card debt is proof enough of that. But now the problem is going to get bigger. In the past, there was only one household to support. Now there will be two. Before, only one telephone bill came at the beginning of the month. Now there will be a second. And so it will go, down the line. If that is the case, how will you be able to manage financially?

As I said, these are real concerns, and there can be no denying them. But that is not the issue. The issue is how the two of you are going to deal with them. But isn't that what lawyers are for? You flatter us too much. Lawyers do not know what is best for you. Nor are they necessarily wise. They are just people who went to law school.

Let me explain what I mean. When I graduated from law school, I was not given what I really wanted. In fact, as the dean was about to hand me the diploma I had worked so hard for, I told him there was something that I wanted more. It was not that I did not consider my diploma to be of value. I just felt that I would be able to be of far more help to those who came to me if I had something else. What I really wanted was a crystal ball and a magic wand, and I told him that if he would give them to me, he could keep my diploma. Needless to say, I did not get what I really wanted. All that I got was a diploma.

My point, of course, is that just because someone is a lawyer does not mean that he (or she) has a magic wand that he can wave that will add to the size of your pie and thereby solve all of your problems. He doesn't. He is only a lawyer, not a magician. What then are lawyers trained to do? There is a well-known Japanese saying that expresses it: "Engineers add to the size of the pie; lawyers just fight over how to divide it."

It is what it is. Letting your fears run rampant and impel you to rush off in a hundred different directions will not change that. All that it will do is cause you to lose sight of it. All that it will do is cause you to panic and turn your life over to lawyers. All that it will do is send you off in the wrong direction.

CHAPTER 21

FEELINGS

Husbands and wives tend to argue out in their divorce the very issues they are unable to resolve in their marriage.

This brings me to the second thing that can tend to take your eye off the mark. It is your feelings.

If there is one thing that all divorcing husbands and wives have in common, it is that they feel too much and understand too little. It is not that they are foolish or lacking in intelligence. In most cases, they are anything but that. It is just that they are much too close to what has happened to them. It is just that the feelings they are experiencing are so urgent and so powerful that they tend to overwhelm them and get by their rational censor.

At almost any other time in your life (your marriage being another exception), your critical faculties would not allow your feelings to get out of hand and take over your life. Nevertheless, the powerful feelings now at play will tend to overwhelm your rational censor and render it inoperative. The irony is that while you are better able to see how this happened when you got married, you are still unable to see it now. As a result, you will tend to give far more credence to your feelings than they deserve.

Obviously, the feelings that you had at the beginning of your marriage were very different from the ones that you are experiencing now. Nevertheless, one thing is the same, and that is that, in both instances, you will tend to take your feelings at face value and not question them. If you feel a certain way, you will assume that you are perfectly justified in feeling that way, and that will be the end of it.

There is little point in going back to the feelings that you had when you got married. They are ancient history. However, it is important to consider the feelings that you are experiencing now, as they will have a very dramatic effect on your ability to address and successfully resolve the practical problems that the two of you now find yourself faced with. The feelings that I am referring to are the feelings of hurt and anger, the sense of loss and disappointment, and sometimes even of betrayal, with which one or both of you are now struggling.

Why do we "manufacture" feelings in the first place? The pleasant feelings that we have act as mirrors of what we are experiencing. We are at peace with ourselves and the world and we experience (manufacture) feelings that mirror that. The unpleasant feelings we experience when our world is out of joint act as a mirror as well. But we manufacture them principally as a shield to protect us from the disarray in our lives. We may not be able to change what is happening to us. We may not even be able to make too much sense of it. But we can at least attempt to defend ourselves from its more damaging effects. In a sense, it is our way of fighting back.

To the extent that we manufacture feelings to protect our integrity, that is healthy. As I said, it is necessary to keep our stories straight, or at least as straight as we can. However, if we cling to those feelings or worse, savor them, they will then become a hindrance rather than a help. Rather than allow us to regain our strength and be able to walk again on our own, these feelings will become a crutch that we will instead lean on. If we are not careful, they may become a prison from which we are unable to escape.

Unfortunately, those feelings will have a more immediate effect. They will impede your ability to sit down and address the practical problems with which the two of you are confronted as a result of the decision that has been made to separate and perhaps divorce.

Most husbands and wives know how destructive their feelings

can be. They also know that the better part of wisdom is to keep them in check—as I say, to keep them beneath the surface. However, there are two problems. The first is that the surface is paper-thin. In fact, it is even thinner than that. The second is that those feelings are dying for expression. Thus, if the two of you were to sit down, particularly on your own, and attempt to address any of the practical problems with which you are faced, there is the real danger that one of you will put his or her finger on one of those weak spots in the surface. If that happens, those feelings, which are dying for expression, will burst forth and overwhelm you. Nor will it make any difference what you are discussing. It could be nothing more consequential than who will keep the teapot. The power of those feelings will be such that they will create such a smoke screen that neither of you will even be able to remember what was at issue. Your common sense would tell you that it would be better to throw the teapot in the garbage than to have this much commotion over it. Nevertheless, once you give free reign to those feelings, all of that will change. It will now become a question of principle.

Just as married couples rarely fight over what they are really arguing about, divorcing couples tend to argue out in their divorce the very issues they were unable to resolve in their marriage. That is why their discussions tend to generate far more heat than light. It is also why they are so unproductive. They are going back and rehashing issues they were unable to resolve in the past that they have even less chance of resolving now. It is no longer the teapot. The teapot has come to represent something else.

I was confronted with this situation a number of years ago. The couple with whom I was working had successfully concluded an agreement involving the division of millions of dollars. They were now down to the wire. They had even resolved the division of most of their personal property (furniture, silverware, dishes, etc.). There was only one issue left, a piano. While the piano had some real value, it was insignificant in terms of the value of what they had already divided. Nor did it seem that either of them had that much emotional attachment to it, though they each advanced reasons why it should remain theirs. Nevertheless, it started to generate a lot of heat. As reality-based as both of them were, I nevertheless began to worry that they might each throw in the towel, scuttle the agreement they had so laboriously and carefully worked out and, if need be, "go down in flames" over the issue of the piano.

I came to realize that the piano was not the real issue. It was something else. They probably wouldn't even have been able to put their finger on what that real issue was, and the piano had just come to represent it. As is always the case, neither of them was happy about what had happened in their lives. Nor did they agree on how they had gotten there. On the contrary, as is again almost always the case, each saw himself (and herself) as being the innocent victim in all of this. Each saw themselves as being where they were because of what the other had done or been unwilling to do. And since this is not where they intended to be or felt they deserved to be, they were each overwhelmed by all of the feelings that I mentioned earlier.

Until this point, they had each managed to keep those feelings in check. At least they had not seriously interfered with the practical matters at hand. Now, however, they were. As irrational as this was, what the husband was telling himself (what was making it so difficult for him to let go of the piano) was that if he let his wife keep it, that meant that he had to accept her explanation of how it was and why it was that the two of them had gotten to this point in their lives, and he would be dammed if he would do that. He would rather go down in flames. And his wife felt the same way. It wasn't the piano. It was what the piano came to represent—the feeling that they had each allowed themselves to attach to it.

What is the moral here? It is that you can either take control of your feelings or your feelings will take control of you. If you are going to be able to successfully address the problems with which you are now faced, you have only one choice. At all costs, you cannot allow your feelings to take control of you. If you do, you are lost.

I want to be clear here. I am not calling into question how you feel. Again, since I have not led your life, it would be very inappropriate for me to pass judgment on how you feel. I would have to be able to put myself in your shoes, and I cannot do that. All that I am saying is that no matter how valid your feelings may be, they have nothing to do with the teapot. In other words, you cannot allow the teapot to become the object of all those feelings. If you do, you risk finding yourself going down the wrong road. If you are not careful, you may even find yourself going down in flames.

Obviously, that is not what you want. Nor is there any point in it. Your critical faculties will tell you that. If you will listen to them, they will tell you something else, namely, that somehow you must get through this. You will not do that, however, if you allow the feelings you are struggling with to get out of hand and take your eye off the mark.

CHAPTER 22

USING ALL THE SMARTS YOU WERE GIVEN

You are going to come across many signposts along the way. Unfortunately, many will point you in the wrong direction.

If there was ever a time in your life when you will need all the smarts you were given, and then some, it is now. Navigating through the difficult waters of your divorce is not going to be easy. On the contrary, it will be one of the most difficult experiences that you will be required to undergo in your life. It will test you as few things ever have or ever will. It will force you to dig deeper than you have ever gone before.

To be sure, you can do what many people do most of the time in their lives, which is to turn on autopilot, sit back and just let things proceed as they will. Nor is there normally very much danger in that. However, there are other times when it will not do just to fly by the seat of your pants, let alone to fall asleep at the wheel. That is when, as now, a storm is brewing. At times like this, you cannot afford just to let yourself be carried along by the current of your emotions. That is the surest recipe for disaster. At times like this, you will have to keep your hands firmly on the wheel, take careful stock of the situation and watch where you are going. At times like these, you are going to have to use all the smarts you were given and then some.

How can you do this? To begin with, you must not accept at face value everything that you hear or are told. You are going to come across many signposts along the way. Unfortunately, many of them will point you in the wrong direction. Before you follow any of them you must stop and ask, "Where does this road—this course of conduct—lead? If I take that first step, what will my husband's or wife's reaction be? Will that improve things or only make them worse?" Most important, you must ask, "Where will it end?" Those are not questions that those who will urge you to go off on your own and resort to self-help will encourage you to ask. They are critical questions, however. Taking the first step and going off on your own is always how it starts. That is always how things begin to get out of control.

If you follow my advice and use all the smarts you were ever given, what will they tell you? They will tell you that, in considering any course of conduct, you must learn to think backward (backward from where you want to be) rather than forward (forward from where you are).

Thinking forward means to take what appears to be the next logical step. If you want to protect yourself, go to the bank and withdraw all of the money on deposit in your joint savings account. Having taken the first logical step, you will then take the next. The only trouble is that you will not have thought out where that logic will bring you. You will certainly not have thought out what your husband's or wife's response to your first step will be. That is the trouble with all of those seemingly logical steps. No one ever really examines their logic—where they inevitably lead. If they did, they would realize that there was really very little logic to them. They are just emotional reactions, not thoughtful actions.

What does it mean to think backward? Ironically, it means to think correctly—to start out by asking yourself where you want to end up and what you will have to do to get there. It also means to ask yourself where you do not want to end up and what you must do to avoid that. You know the answer to this. You don't want to end up starting the Third World War just because you are getting a divorce.

Why, if their common sense is enough to tell them this, do

so many divorcing couples find themselves where they do not want to be—embroiled in adversarial divorce proceedings? It is because they do not use all the smarts they were given. It is because they allow the circumstances of their divorce to dull their rational censor. It is because they become so overwhelmed that they take their eye off the mark.

CHAPTER 23

BUSINESS AS USUAL

Resorting to self-help doesn't help. It only makes things worse.

We all know what business as usual means. It means continuing to do what you have always done. If, in the past, the two of you deposited your paychecks into a joint account, why would you change that while the two of you are deciding what will happen in the future? Similarly, if in the past it was the custom, as it is in most marriages, for one of you to write out the checks to pay the phone bill and the electric bill, why would you change that either? There is no reason to, which is why the rule should be business as usual.

Why is it so important not to break that rule? Because when you do that, you begin to "position" yourself, or at least that is how your husband or wife will see it. Then he will begin to position himself, as well. When that happens, it is literally impossible to get it right. On the contrary, it will always come out wrong.

Consider this. You and your husband or wife have a joint savings account with a balance of $10,000 in it. What should you do? If you follow the principle of business as usual, you will do nothing today that you didn't do yesterday.

That, of course, is not the advice that you will get from your Greek Chorus of well-wishers. What they will tell you is that you have to protect yourself. How can you do that? By going to the bank and withdrawing all the money. There is only one problem. If you follow their advice, that leaves you a thief, and you are really not a thief. What will be your Greek Chorus' answer? It will be that it is better to be a thief with the money than a fool without it, which is what you will be if you allow your husband or wife to take it out first.

What is the answer to this dilemma? This is something that I struggled with in the years that I was in practice in the adversarial world of divorce. My clients weren't thieves, but I didn't want to leave them fools either. My advice was that they should go to the bank and either withdraw half of the money in the account and then instruct the bank to change the account into the other's name alone, or better yet, to freeze the account so that neither of them would be able to withdraw any of the funds without the other's permission. Certainly that would be "protecting" my client. More importantly, it would do it in a way that would not leave my client either a thief or a fool.

What thanks did my clients get for acting in such a responsible manner? None at all. That is not how their husbands or wives viewed what they had done. Rather, they viewed it as a declaration of war, and invariably their response was, "I would never have done that." It made no difference whether that was true or not. That is how they saw it. That is how they will always see it if you stop doing business as usual and resort to self-help.

But it gets worse. When you break the rule of business as usual, one step necessarily leads to another. You think that you are only doing one thing, and that it will end there. But there is no end. As I said, for every tit there will be a tat, *ad infinitum*. After a while, neither of you will even be able to remember where it began. Nor will it make any difference. That is always what happens when husbands and wives break the rule of business as usual and resort to self-help. It doesn't help. It only makes things worse.

That is why it is so important to commit yourself to the proposition that it is business as usual. Otherwise, things will inevitably get out of hand. Contrary to what others may tell you, it is not possible for you to maintain control alone. Since what is happening involves the two of you, it is going to take the two of you to do that. That, of course, means that the two of you will have to sit down and, despite what will inevitably be your differences of opinion and your different views of the situation, find a way to address the problems that you now find yourselves faced with.

To be sure, in most instances you will not be able to do that on your own, which is why you will need help. When you get that help, there will be time enough to do what the two of you have to do. More importantly, you will do it together. Until then, it must be business as usual.

PART IV

The Fork in the Road

CHAPTER 24

THE OTHER ROAD

Divorces should be conducted with dignity, but they should cost no more than dignity requires.

I said that there is another road the two of you can take. It is time to be more specific. That road has been given a name; it is called *divorce mediation.*

Before I tell you what divorce mediation is, it would perhaps be better to tell you what it is not. This will avoid confusion. It is not marriage counseling. Its purpose is not to explore or address the problems in your marriage that have brought you to where you are. Its purpose is to address the problems that the two of you now find yourselves faced with as a result of your decision, or the decision of one of you, to separate and divorce.

It is not for a particular class of people. You do not have to be rich. You do not have to be poor. It is for anyone and everyone, regardless of their economic circumstances. Similarly, it is not for a particular kind of person. You do not have to fit a certain description, such as being fair-minded or perfectly reasonable, anymore than not being fair minded or perfectly reasonable is a pre-requisite to being a candidate for adversarial divorce proceedings. Thus, while it would be better if the two of you were able to talk easily with one another, it is not necessary. I have worked with any number of husbands and wives who, though they were literally unable to discuss anything outside my office, were able to talk with one another without any difficulty when the three of us met together. That, again, is the importance of context. What is not possible in one context is possible in another. It is not just for people who have worked out most if not all of the issues that they find themselves faced with. It is also for people who have worked out none of them. Finally, it is not better suited to deal with certain types of problems, such as children, than with others, such as money. It will help the two of you address all of the problems that you find yourselves confronted with at this point in your lives.

I said that divorce mediation is not for a particular group of people. I must correct myself. While it is for other couples as well, it is particularly suited for those who are concerned about their children—those who want to shelter their children from the worst effects of their divorce. If your divorce will be difficult for you, it will be difficult for your children, as well. Nor is this only the case if they are young. Children of all ages are affected by their parents' divorce. They are just affected differently.

Divorce mediation was born of this understanding. In fact, it was born in response to the terrible damage that children inevitably suffer when their parents resort to adversarial divorce proceedings. Children need the support of both a mother and a father. Employing a procedure that inevitably makes adversaries of the two of you does not promote that. On the contrary, it will only make it more difficult for the two of you to minister to your children's needs at this critical time. It will also leave your children in the one place where they do not belong—in the middle. Worse, in protracting the conclusion of your divorce, as it inevitably does, it will only leave them there that much longer.

You can avoid that by going off together down the other road. In fact, this is one of the principal reasons why divorcing couples employ divorce mediation. They want to properly finish the job that they began. To do that, they know that they must still be able to work together. To do that, they know that they cannot allow their divorce to get out of hand. To do that, they know that they must bring it to a speedy conclusion. That is the promise of mediation.

There is one other important characteristic of mediation, and that is that a mediator does not have the power to make any decisions. In other words, unlike a judge or an arbitrator, he or she will not listen to each of you and then make a determination that will be binding upon you. Rather, a mediator's purpose is to help the two of you make those decisions yourselves. His objective is to assist the two of you to conclude an agreement that both of you feel you can live with, not one that he feels he can live with.

Though there are certain things that a mediator does not do, there is a great deal that he or she does do. He will provide you with the relevant information that you will need in order to make the important decisions that you now find yourselves faced with. He will point out the different options that you have and courses of action that you may wish to consider. He will tell you based on his experience what things work better and what things do not work at all. He will make suggestions and propose solutions when you get stuck. Finally, he will provide you with his calm and balanced judgment when the two of you need it. He just will not take over your lives or legislate your decisions. That is why you will not have to worry that the mediation may go in a direction you had not expected or end up in a place where you do not want to be. In fact, that is one of the greatest virtues of divorce mediation. Whatever your worst fears may be, if they should come to pass, or should the mediation go in a direction you had not expected or intended, you are always free to get up and leave.

The same is not true, however, if you each go off on your own, resort to self-help, and commence adversarial divorce proceedings. You will have all the control there, too, until you set it in motion. Once you have done that, however, it will quickly take on a life of its own. But it will be worse than that. It will be like a run away train, and there will be no way to stop it. Though it is your two lives that are in issue, you will nevertheless find yourselves but bit players, consigned to the wings of the drama. Even your two lawyers, who will appear center stage, will have very little control over what will happen. In allowing the proceeding to take on a life of its own, you will have violated the first principle, which is that it is the two of you who should control the events in your lives, not the events in your lives control you.

That is the critical distinction between divorce mediation and adversarial divorce proceedings. The two of you will go off together, rather than separately on your own. Your first meeting will be a "get-to-know-you meeting." At this point the two of you have not decided to employ this process, let alone to retain the services of this particular mediator. You are just going to learn more about your options, to get to know the mediator to see whether you feel comfortable with him or her, and to ask whatever questions you have. After you have left and the two of you have had an opportunity to talk on your own, you will then decide whether this is the procedure you wish to employ and the mediator with whom you want to work. You may want to meet with more than one mediator before you make that decision.

Divorce mediation has certain other very important advantages. It does not take forever. While it obviously varies from couple to couple, most couples get to the point where it is time to start drafting their agreement in a relatively short period of time. In my practice, I schedule weekly meetings of an hour and a half and usually get to that point in four to five sessions. If the couple has been married for only a few years and do not have children, I will normally conclude the matter in one or perhaps two meetings. In fact, my experience is that most couples will conclude an agreement from beginning to end in less time than it would have taken their separate lawyers just to exchange information, let alone make an initial proposal to one another.

While everything costs something, unlike adversarial divorce proceedings, divorce mediation does not cost a king's ransom. Cost is a function of time. The longer it takes, the more it costs. That, too, is one of the important benefits of divorce mediation. Couples faced with the prospect of their divorce need all of the money they have. They cannot afford to squander it. After all, the object is for them to save their money to put their own children through college, not to put their lawyer's children through college. That is exactly what you will be doing, however, if you each go off on your own and resort to self-help.

Divorce mediation has two other very important characteristics. The first, as I noted earlier, is the context in which the discussions between the two of you will take place. Inevitably, husbands and wives are overwhelmed by the prospects of their divorce. Their mediation sessions, which are often the only place where they are able to talk together productively, tend to represent a safe haven.

Perhaps mediation's most important virtue, however, is that it prevents things from getting out of hand. Those with whom I now work have none of the protection that our adversarial legal system supposedly provides them when the other turns to self-help—applies financial pressure to force a settlement by not paying the mortgage or utilities, or applies psychological pressure by withholding the children. They have also taken the chance of not doing any of the things that lawyers representing clients in adversarial divorce proceedings counsel them to do—run to the bank and grab the money, cancel the credit cards, etc. Ironically, they do not need the protection. None of these things ever happen. A divorce lawyer could not possibly understand this. Living in the adversarial world that he does, where the self-fulfilling prophecy turns husbands and wives into adversaries, he would not be able to imagine it otherwise. Nevertheless, it is so.

I have assisted thousands of couples down that other road. In literally no case have I had someone come to me complaining about receiving notice that the heat was going to be turned off or that the mortgage was going to be foreclosed. It doesn't happen. That just isn't the way couples who go down that road act. That is not how they feel they need to act. Nor, since the rule is not "anything goes," do they feel that this is an appropriate way to act. But there is more to it. They do not have a lawyer to hide behind who will make excuses for them if they do resort to self-help. Rather, in the context in which their discussions take place, they will have to face their husband or wife on their own. There is no profit in that. Nor is there any point in it. That is why it literally never happens.

CHAPTER 25

THE LOWLY COIN

Never throw away a bad idea unless you have a better one.

I said earlier that the problem that you now find yourself faced with is the same problem that literally every married couple who gets to this point in their lives is faced with, namely, how are each of you going to be able to manage financially in the future and what obligation should one of you have to the other (and to your children) to be concerned with how he or she will be able to do that?

Let us suppose for the moment that the two of you have very different opinions as to what the answer to that question (or any other question that you have to decide) should be. How will you decide it? You will have to employ a procedure. The question is, which one?

Husbands and wives don't generally give very much thought to this. Rather, they assume that they must turn to lawyers for that purpose and leave it at that. Obviously, that is not your only choice. There are many others. Before you make that decision, it would make sense to consider your options. After all, you want to choose the best one.

One way you could decide it would be to toss a coin. Heads you win, tails he or she wins. Needless to say, you would not feel comfortable doing that. In fact, you would not take me very seriously were I to suggest it. After all, the two of you are talking about very important matters. I agree.

Before you discard the lowly coin, however, I would like to

say a word in defense of the coin toss. In fact, I will argue that it is probably the most efficient dispute resolution procedure that has ever been devised. It is cheap. Since you undoubtedly have a quarter in your pocket or purse, it won't cost you anything. It is quick. It will only take a few seconds. And it is as clear as the nose on your face. There are no ifs, ands or buts. It is either heads or tails. I could even point out that it is used to make many important decisions, such as which of the two teams in the Super Bowl will get the right to decide whether to kick off or receive the ball.

Nevertheless, I doubt that you will be persuaded. I understand that. You do not want just any answer. You want the right answer. How can a coin guarantee that when it is simply a matter of chance? It can't. I will therefore have to look for some better procedure. Before I do that, however, I want to point out something. If you reject the lowly coin despite its obvious virtues, then it doesn't make any sense to substitute another procedure unless it at least has all of those virtues and more. Otherwise, you would be better off using a coin.

Let us consider some other possibilities. You could decide the issue by engaging in a contest. I could even suggest an intellectual one, such as a game of chess. Nevertheless, I doubt that you would be any better satisfied. After all, you do not want to make a game of this. You want to make some sense of it, and any procedure you employ should be guaranteed to do that. That is why leaving it to chance or to a game, even one of skill, will not do.

Ironically, unless the two of you sit down and decide this on your own (or with the help of someone), that is exactly what you will do. You will turn to lawyers and allow them to decide it by engaging in a legal contest. To be sure, that is not how lawyers will describe it. If they did, you would never turn to them. Nor, unfortunately, will you see that this is what they are doing. The blazing light of the lofty abstractions that lawyers invoke will blind you to that. The one thing that those lofty abstractions cannot do, however, is change anything. You will still have committed yourselves to deciding the important issues in your life by engaging in a contest. Nor will it make any difference that the contest you employ is a game of legal chess.

Perhaps you can better understand what I meant when I said earlier that you will come across signposts along the way that will send you off in the wrong direction, that you cannot take everything you see and hear at face value, and that you will have to use all the smarts you were given. The signpost that will send the two of you down the wrong road will lead you to believe that you will be employing a rational procedure guaranteed to leave you with the right answer to your questions. It isn't. It is only a game. It is no better than the lowly coin. In fact, it does not have a single one of a coin's virtues.

CHAPTER 26

THE TABLE AND THE TABLE CLOTH

Never watch the mouth. Always watch the feet.

You have been persuaded that it serves no useful purpose to make a game of this. Rather, you want to make some sense of it, at least as much sense as you can. That is what you will be doing if you go off together down the other road.

To explain this, I am going to employ a metaphor that I use with couples who come to me for help. Again, I use the small round table we are sitting at to make my point. However, I now add a tablecloth. I ask them to imagine that they have a dining room table and a tablecloth. The table represents the problem. The tablecloth represents the resources that they have to cover the problem.

In the past, there used to be enough, or barely enough, to cover the table. But they have now gone out and bought a new, larger table, and when they put their old tablecloth on it, they find that they have a problem. It used to fit, or barely fit. But now it is too small for the table.

This, of course, is exactly your problem. How are the two of you going to solve it? As you will find, there are only two procedures that you can employ. In the terms that I have put it, there are two different roads that you can go down.

In making that choice, and particularly in listening to how that choice will be presented to you, it is critical that you remember something. Never watch the mouth. Always watch the feet. In other words, it is not how someone *describes* what he is doing, but what he is *actually* doing, that is important.

If you each go off on your own, resort to self-help, and retain separate lawyers, what will your two lawyers do with the tablecloth that is too small for the table? What their mouths will be saying, of course, is that they are protecting your legal rights and getting what is fair and equitable for you. That is not what their feet will be doing, however. Their feet will be engaged in a tug-of-war over the tablecloth, one of your lawyers pulling as hard as he or she can on one end and the other pulling just as hard on the other. Will the object of their efforts really be to get what is fair, as their mouths insist? Put another way, is that really the word that would come to mind to describe what you are watching them do? Of course not. Despite what their mouths may be saying, neither of your lawyers will be using their efforts to get what is fair for you. Rather, what they will be trying to do is get what is best for you. And in the tug-of-war that they will be engaged in, what is best for you is to get as much of the table cloth as they can and to give up as little of it as they have to.

There is something else about a tug-of-war that it is important for you to keep in mind. Someone always gets dragged through the dirt. To be sure, you might answer by saying, "Yes, but we are very fortunate. There is no dirt here." That may be true. Nevertheless, wait until your lawyers start scratching around. Divorce lawyers have the rather strange idea that the best way to make a case for their own client is to muddy their client's husband or wife. It really doesn't make a good case for anyone. It just leaves a lot of people coming away feeling and looking very dirty.

What will happen if you go down the road that I am recommending? You will deal with the problem very differently. You will direct your efforts at spreading the tablecloth around the table in such a way so that each of you will be left with a portion of it to cover your end of the problem and so that neither of you will be left too much more exposed than the other. In other words, your will direct your efforts towards solving your problem, not making a game of it. You do not need a legal education to know that this is a far more responsible way to deal with your problem. All you need is your common sense.

Does this mean that the two of you will see the problem in the same way? I am not suggesting that. None of us is able to completely put ourselves in someone else's shoes. The two of you will not even look at the table from the same perspective. One of you will see it from here and the other will see it from there. But that does not mean that you are not sitting around the same table—that you do not have a common problem. To be sure, you may not see it as being a common problem. And your Greek Chorus of well-wishers will certainly not encourage you to see it as that. Nevertheless, it is.

I must make something clear. If I am encouraging you to deal with your problem in this way, it is not because I am standing on principle or responding to some higher moral vision, and you would terribly misunderstand me if you thought that. Rather, it is because I see the problem in very practical terms. It is because, if my years of experience have taught me anything, it is that to be of help means to solve the problem for both of you, not just for one of you—certainly not for one of you at the expense of the other.

But, as I said, to solve the problem for both of you means, of necessity, to leave you with an agreement that you both feel you can live with. For if either of you come away feeling that you have been left with an agreement that you cannot live with, it will not be worth the paper it is written on. Rather, it will just be the battlefield on which you will wage your future wars. There is no profit in that. Again, it has nothing to do with principle. It is just common sense.

That, unfortunately, is the sad legacy that has been bequeathed to those who have gone off on their own, resorted to self-help, and turned to adversarial divorce proceedings. Ironically, divorce lawyers know this. They even have an expression for it. It is: "Divorces never end." They never end because, rather than attempting to solve the serious problem that divorcing husbands and wives find themselves faced with, divorce lawyers just make a game of it. The result is that when one of the parties walks off the playing field congratulating himself or herself on how well he has done—how much of the tablecloth he or she has come away with—there is a tap on his or her shoulder. When they turn around, there is their husband or wife, who says, "It is not over. That was just the end of round one."

Characterizing the tug-of-war as being about your legal rights doesn't change this. It just prevents you from seeing it. It just takes your eye off the mark. It gets you to watch the mouth rather than the feet. Never let yourself be fooled by the mouth. Always watch the feet.

CHAPTER 27

REALITY

It behooves us to be realistic because we are condemned to wake up each morning and rub our noses up against reality.

Without doubt, we can paint pretty pictures in the sky of what it would be like to live in an imaginary world of perfection, one in which everything is as it should be, all of our wishes are granted and nothing is ever denied to us. But we do not live in such a world and never will. Rather, we live in a very imperfect world, one of constraint and human limitation, and in such a world compromises will have to be made. That was true in your marriage and it will be true in your divorce as well. Why would you expect it to be otherwise? Thus, if you see any signposts along the way that tell you otherwise, don't be fooled. Getting divorced is serious business. You can't afford to listen to fairy tales.

If you each go off on your own, resort to self-help, and retain separate lawyers, that is not what you will be told. Lawyers do not live in the real world. They live in an unreal world of fantasy, a world in which no one is ever allowed to make a mistake. If they do—lawyers call that negligence—they will pay for it. Since we live in an imperfect world in which everyone makes mistakes, some lawyers have been able to make an industry out of this. They call themselves "negligence lawyers."

Since divorce lawyers believe that the world they live in should be a perfect world, they insist that everything that takes place there must measure up to the level of perfection. This is especially true of the negotiations that will take place between the two of you. (In the past, the two of you used to discuss things with one another. Once you retain divorce lawyers, however, everything becomes a negotiation.) Thus, divorce lawyers will insist that the two of you must be given a perfect setting in which to conduct your negotiations. Lawyers refer to this as a "level playing field" and it is one of their favorite metaphors. They are forever asking, "But was it a level playing field?"

Since we do not live in a perfect world, none of us has ever been given a level playing field—a perfect set of conditions. In fact, if we refused to leave our homes in the morning and go off on our appointed tasks unless we were first guaranteed a level playing field, very little of the world's work would ever get done.

If the truth be told, there are no level playing fields in a lawyer's world either. It is just all lawyer talk. The idea that two lawyers, each of whom is doing everything that he (or she) can to slant the playing field in his own client's favor, will nevertheless end up with a perfectly level one, is worse than legal mythology. It is legal nonsense.

Divorce lawyers also love to talk about what is "fair" and "equitable." These are amongst their favorite words. Again, what they suggest is that, though your marriage may not have been fair, your divorce will be. Don't be fooled. If a divorce lawyer could, in your divorce, make your husband (or wife) the very person that you felt he never was in your marriage, you wouldn't have to divorce him. But he is not going to be able to do that. That would require a magic wand. Unfortunately, he wasn't given a magic wand when he graduated from law school. All that he was given was a fancy piece of paper—a diploma.

The moral is that it is not possible to escape the world of constraint and human limitation that we live in. It is not possible to avoid having to make compromise with life. That being the case, it makes sense to somehow find the way to accept that.

To be sure, there will be those who will suggest otherwise. They will hold up a picture of a world in which everyone gets what they deserve and no one is forced to make compromises. They will also tell you that it can be yours. Don't be taken in by it. It is not a picture of the real world. It is a picture of an unreal world. It is a picture of a world of fantasy.

CHAPTER 28

A LITTLE SECRET

Difficult people are not stronger. They are just rigid.

There is something that you will not find in the picture that a divorce lawyer will hold up to you. It is one of the little secrets about adversarial divorce proceedings. Those proceedings favor unhealthy people. For the same reason, they put healthy people at a disadvantage.

There are two necessary components in any definition of mental health. They are the ability to adapt and the ability to make compromise with life. Unhealthy people are not able to do that. That is why they are unhealthy. Unhealthy people are not stronger, as the conventional wisdom would have it. They are just rigid and inflexible. They are living proof of the adage that a branch breaks where it cannot bend. If need be, they would rather go down in flames than to make compromise with life. The way that they will defend this, of course, is to insist that it is a matter of principle, and there can be no compromise with principle.

That is why, if you are basically healthy, you will be at a disadvantage if you turn to adversarial divorce proceedings. As I said, those proceedings tend to take on a life of their own. Worse, they become like a run away train, and there is only one way to stop it. That is for the two of you to come to an agreement. You will want to do that. You will even be willing to make compromises for that purpose. That is because you are basically healthy.

If your husband or wife is also basically healthy, they, too, will be willing to compromise in order to get it done. That will not be the case, however, if they are unhealthy. Then it will become a question of principle, and they will rather go down in flames than compromise their principle. Nor will it make any difference to them if they bring you, your children and even themselves down in the process. They will see it to the bitter end regardless of the cost.

Am I saying that if you go down the road I am recommending that your husband or wife will now miraculously become reasonable? No. Difficult people are difficult no matter where you put them. Nevertheless, they will be more difficult or less difficult depending upon where you put them. Again, that is the importance of context.

You will therefore have to choose. You know that if you turn to adversarial divorce proceedings, you will be choosing a context that favors unhealthy people and puts you at a disadvantage. That is because it encourages unhealthy people to believe that their refusal to bend and make compromise with life is a virtue rather than a vice. That is because it encourages them to see their stubbornness as a strength rather than as a weakness. Worse, it gives them a champion to defend their intransigence, as unreasonable as it may be.

If you go down the other road, you will be choosing a context that does just the opposite. Again, this is not to say that context will change a lion into a lamb. Nevertheless, because it will not turn your divorce into a contest in which the winner takes all, it will not cause your husband or wife to feel that their only hope is in acting like a lion. Rather, it will encourage them to see that it makes far more sense to conclude an agreement that works for both of you, not just for one of you alone.

That is why you really have no choice. The road that I am recommending may not be a certainty, but the wrong road is. It is certain to be a disaster. Given a choice between a risk and a certainty, a healthy person would never hesitate.

CHAPTER 29

IS IT FAIR?

One cannot expect perfect solutions to imperfect problems.

Is it fair that someone who is married to a decent, generous person will fare better in their divorce than someone who is married to a husband or wife who is the opposite? Obviously not. But then, no one ever said life was fair. If it was, you would not be getting a divorce in the first place. In fact, particularly if you are the one initiating the divorce, you may well feel this was the problem in your marriage—that it was anything but fair and you were forever being short-changed. But why would you expect in your divorce the very thing that was denied to you in your marriage?

One answer, of course, would be to say that this is exactly why you are getting a divorce—so that you won't have to come out on the short end of the stick one more time. Nevertheless, until you conclude your divorce, you are still married to your husband or wife, which means that you must continue do business with him or her. Thus, to get a divorce (in your terms perhaps, to be rid of him or her), it may be necessary for you to come out on the short end of the stick one more time. As difficult as this will be, it is important that you come to terms with this reality—find a way to accept it and keep your story straight at the same time.

Admittedly, that poses a problem for you. How can you accept coming out on the short end of the stick, even one more time? Rather than attempt to answer that question, I am going to suggest that you ask a different question, hopefully a better one. If we lived in a perfect world, it wouldn't make any difference what question we asked. In the imperfect world in which we live, however, the questions that we ask are critical. Ask the wrong question and you will get the wrong answer. As I said before, if you want a better answer, you will have to ask a better question.

Let me help you do that. Imagine that you have come home at the end of the day and find that your son is not there. On the refrigerator door is a note which says: "Your son has been kidnapped and if you want him returned you will have to raise $250,000. You will get a call tomorrow telling you where to deliver the money. If you call the police, you will never see your son again."

What will you do? You could sit down and ask yourself meaningless questions, such as whether it is fair for someone to kidnap your son, and equally pointless ones, such as whether if you give in to the kidnapper's demands, are you only rewarding criminal behavior and perhaps even encouraging it? You would be better served spending your time and energy trying to raise the money. There will be time enough for all these questions (if anyone is still interested) once you have secured your son's release.

I doubt that there will be any disagreement between us here. But why should it be any different when it comes to your divorce? Particularly if you are the one who wants the divorce, you may well feel that your life is being held for ransom. You may even feel that you are drowning in your marriage, and you desperately want your life back.

Do not misunderstand me. I am not suggesting that you should pay a king's ransom to get your life back. You must keep your story straight, and if the price that you have to pay is too high, it will be far more difficult for you to do that. There are consequences in that. What I am suggesting is the following:

First, that compromises will have to be made. We all pay for what we want. Sometimes, we even pay for what we don't want. That would not be the case if we lived in a perfect world. But we don't. We live in a very imperfect one.

Second, don't turn what is only a compromise into a king's ransom. That is what happens when you allow yourself to get carried away by your emotions. Then it is no longer a compromise. It becomes a question of principle (a king's ransom), and there is no compromising principle.

Third, as hard as it will be, when your husband or wife looks at things differently than you do, try to remember that he or she also has a story that he is trying to keep straight. You can characterize him as simply being stubborn or unreasonable. You may even be right. But being right doesn't change anything. It is also possible that your judgments are just your convenient way of avoiding having to acknowledge or accept the needs expressed in his point of view. You may not like his point of view. He may not like yours. But that is still how he feels. It was the reality in your marriage. It will be the reality in your divorce.

Fourth, do not pay for anything twice. If you lose a pen, it may cost you $30 or $40 to replace it. If on top of that, you aggravate yourself over the fact that you have lost it, you will now have made two payments, not one. In other words, if you are forced to make a necessary compromise to get it done, leave it at that.

Fifth, do not pay the price of keeping your story straight at the cost of bending your life out of shape. That is what happens when people get mad, get up and, without looking where they are going, head off down the wrong road. It is no less the wrong road just because you go down it in anger.

Sixth, don't make it more difficult for yourself by asking the wrong questions, such as "Is it fair?" Those who encourage you to ask these questions would have you believe that your divorce takes place in a world different from your marriage. It doesn't. It takes place in the same world. If you will have to deal with your husband or wife in your divorce just as you had to deal with him or her in your marriage, how can it be a different world?

Finally, remember that if you want a better answer you will have to ask a better question. Without doubt, you will be forced to make compromises to conclude an agreement with your husband or wife. If that is the case, do not make it more difficult for yourself by asking, "Is it fair that I should be forced to give in to him or her again?" There is no profit in that question. You lose either way. Ask a better question. Ask, "Is it worth it to be done with this? Is it worth it to get back my life?" There is an answer to that question. More importantly, it is an answer that will allow you to keep your story straight without bending your life out of shape.

CHAPTER 30

A BETTER YARDSTICK

It is your life. Don't measure it by someone else's yardstick.

In suggesting that you ask a better question, I am suggesting something else as well. It is that you use a better yardstick to judge the decisions that you will make in your divorce. In fact, one of the messages of this book is that you must make your decisions based on the realities of the world we live in, not based on a world of fantasy.

If you did that, what yardstick would you use? Understandably, you would like the agreement you conclude to be one that will meet your needs, and in many ways it will. Nevertheless, since the tablecloth will inevitably be too small for the table, it will not be possible for your agreement to meet all of your needs completely. You will therefore have to find another yardstick, one that you can employ when it doesn't. I am going to recommend one. It is the one that asks, "Is it an agreement that I feel I can live with?"

Admittedly, that yardstick does not have the luster or appeal of a divorce lawyer's yardstick. There are two reasons for this. The first, and most obvious, is that it is not emblazoned with the lofty abstractions that lawyers engrave on theirs. In other words, it does not ask whether the agreement is "fair," "just," or "equitable." The second is that it is a negative yardstick rather than a positive one. It does not ask whether your agreement measures up to the highest possible standard. More modestly, it asks whether it falls below an acceptable level.

Why is it important to use a negative rather than a positive yardstick? Because you do not need a yardstick when your agreement meets all of your needs, hopes and expectations. You only need one when it doesn't. By definition, the yardstick that asks whether it is fair, or just, or equitable cannot do that, because it is a test that passes only perfect agreements, not agreements that are less than perfect. But it is not possible for the two of you to be left with a perfect agreement—one that meets all of your needs. That is because it can only meet all of the needs of one of you at the expense of meeting little or none of the needs of the other.

Does that mean that if you employ the yardstick I am recommending, the question of whether it is fair, just or equitable will never be asked? Of course it will. After all, you will not be able to live with an agreement if you feel that it is unfair, unjust or inequitable. Those judgments are still relevant. However, they will be made differently.

What is the difference? To begin with, the yardstick that asks the question whether it is an agreement that you feel you can live with is a more realistic one. It does not ask whether your agreement is a perfect one. Rather, it asks whether it is acceptable even if it is not perfect. In short, it does not come from a world of fantasy that we do not live in, and never will. It comes from the real world of constraint and human limitation in which we lead our lives.

Second, the yardstick I am recommending is your yardstick. It asks whether an agreement is acceptable to you, not to someone else. Nor do you have to go to law school to learn how to apply it. You have been using it all of your life.

But wouldn't you like your agreement to measure up to a lawyer's positive yardstick? Of course you would. Who wouldn't? However, you must be careful here. There is a price to be paid in making the mistake of substituting a lawyer's yardstick for your own. It is to allow yourself to be sent on a fool's errand. It is to be given false levels of expectation that will inevitably be followed by equivalent levels of disappointment. That is the sad legacy that has been bequeathed to all those who have bought into legal mythology. They were not left with a perfect agreement. It just took them forever to get a very imperfect one.

But don't take my word for it. You must know someone who went down that road or, better yet, is still in the middle of it. Find out for yourself. All you have to do is ask them some simple questions: How long have you been at it? How far have you gotten? How much has it cost you so far? Then ask them one last question: Are the relations between you and your husband or wife better or worse?

Ironically, you don't have to ask any of those questions. You already know the answers.

CHAPTER 31

GETTING IT RIGHT—GETTING IT DONE

To get it right means to get it done.
To fail to get it done is always to get it wrong.

When separating and divorcing husbands and wives sit down and attempt to conclude an agreement, they invariably find themselves faced with a problem. Moreover, this is true whichever road they go down. That problem is that part of them wants to get it done and another part of them wants to get it right. Why is this a problem? Because to settle for what they are able to get—getting it done—means to give up attempting to get what they want and think they deserve. But to hold out for what they want and think they deserve—getting it right—means not to be able to get it done. Their problem is that they don't want to be forced to make that choice. They want both.

As you will find, that will be your problem as well. Your desire to get it right and your desire to get it done will inevitably be in conflict with one another. Your husband (or wife) may also very much want to get it done, even if it is not as pressing for him as it is for you. Unfortunately, he is going to have a different opinion as to what would measure up and pass that test. That is because he will use a different yardstick than you to do the measuring.

The reason why these two conflicting goals will create a problem for you is that they are both understandable. Going through your divorce will be a very difficult experience. Aside from the personal disruptions that it will cause in your life, it will force you to ask so many questions to which there are no adequate answers. Understandably, you will want to get it done and put it all behind you. But it is also important for you to get it right or, to be more accurate, not to get it wrong. Aside from the reality that you will have to come out of this being able to manage financially, it is going to create a serious problem for you if you get it wrong. It will make it that much more difficult for you to bring some closure to all of this and get on with your life.

Divorce lawyers, of course, will suggest otherwise. That is why so many husbands and wives turn to them. They are taken in by the implied promise that if they go down that road they can have both. What they fail to see is that divorce lawyers never talk about getting it done. Or to be more accurate, even if they do talk about getting it done, that is not one of their priorities. Their only interest is in getting it right. The irony is that they don't get it right—certainly not as they see it. All that they do is fail to get it done. Since getting it done is not one of their priorities, it is never given equal representation.

Obviously, you do not want your divorce to drag on interminably just so that lawyers can engage in long philosophical discussions going nowhere as to what is ultimately fair or just in the world. That is too costly. A lawyer's fees are like those of a taxi driver. You not only pay for every mile—you even pay when the cab isn't moving. It is also too time-consuming. Getting it done may not be important to a divorce lawyer, but it is to you.

What then is the answer? Again, it is to use all the smarts you were given. In this case, it is to see something that a divorce lawyer's lofty abstractions disable you from seeing. To get it right means to get it done and to fail to get it done, as divorce lawyers invariably do, is always to get it wrong. There are two goals, not one, and you cannot afford to let a divorce lawyer's lofty abstractions blind you to this.

There is something else that you must do, and that is accept the reality that it is not possible to get it right, because there is no right. I appreciate that this may run up against everything that you believe and have been told. Nevertheless, it is true. The fact that no two lawyers can ever agree on what is right should be sufficient proof of this. If you understand this, then you will realize that your more modest object should be to avoid getting it wrong.

In this regard, it is important to keep in mind that the term "right" has a very different meaning to a lawyer than it does to you. When a lawyer talks about what is right, he is talking about what will happen in a court of law. When you talk about what is right, you are talking about what took place in your marriage. You are talking about the injustices that you feel you were made to suffer, and perhaps even what you believe was taken away from you in your life. You are talking about the "truth" of what took place in your marriage.

The trouble is that there is no "truth" about your marriage, certainly no "one truth." To be sure, there are a lot of little truths. But they do no add up to the *Truth*. To be more accurate, you and your husband (or wife) will add them up very differently. That is because the truths that we are talking about are not purely factual truths, such as that the two of you were married on a certain date, at a particular place. They are emotionally laden truths, disputes as to who caused what. Unfortunately, these are not truths in the conventional sense. Rather, they are points of view—organizing principles that each of you will employ to explain what has taken place in your marriage. The problem is not just that these points of view will be different. It is that, since each of you will pick out different truths, and ignore or slight what to the other will be most important, each of you will have a very different picture and, therefore, understanding of your marriage. That is what I meant when I said that, though couples with whom I work may have been married to one another, they come to me with different histories of their marriage. They are literally each reporting the history of a different marriage.

How, then, are you going to resolve this conflict between your desire to get it right and to get it done? To do that you will have to keep two things in mind. First, the purpose of your divorce is not to right all of the wrongs, whether real or imagined, that you feel you were made to suffer in your marriage. It is to end your marriage. Don't be misled by the signposts you come across along the way that suggest otherwise.

Second, your marriage and divorce do not take place in different worlds. They take place in the same world. Thus, as compromises had to be made in one, so too will they have to be made in the other. All of the talk about what is right and just and fair that divorce lawyers forever indulge in does not change that. It just prevents you from being able to see it.

CHAPTER 32

LEGAL RIGHTS—LEGAL RULES

If you want an agreement that looks exactly like the one you will get if you go to court, then you will have to go to court to get it.

I want to tell you something about the law. I call it a short course in the law. Its purpose is not to fill your head with a lot of useless legal information. Rather, it is to get you to see the law more realistically. It is to get you to see the law, not as you have been conditioned to see it, as representing your "legal rights," but far more modestly, as simply a set of legal rules. It is also to help you better understand how lawyers employ those legal rules and for what purpose.

To do that, I am going to contrast the rules that lawyers apply with those that mathematicians apply. In both cases, they are applied for a purpose, namely, to answer a question. In both cases, we assume that the answer that we will be given will be the right one. That is why we have faith in those rules. Mathematical rules justify our faith. Contrary to what you have been brought up to believe, however, legal rules do not. There is absolutely no basis for your faith in legal rules. As you will find, it is nothing but blind faith.

Before I address this, I want to return to something that I said earlier, which was that the problem that the two of you now find yourselves faced with is how each of you is going to be able to manage financially in the future. This problem raises the question of what obligation, if any, should one of you have to the other to be concerned with how he or she (and your children, if you have any) will be able to do that? That is your problem. It is obviously not a legal problem. It is a practical life problem.

If, instead of deciding this on your own, the two of you turn to adversarial divorce proceedings and go off to court, a judge has been charged with the responsibility of answering that question for you. Since we do not want judges to do that based on their own personal opinions or value systems, let alone their own biases, our state legislatures enacted our various divorce laws to provide them with a set of rules to apply for that purpose. That is what our divorce laws represent. In fact, that is all that they represent—an arbitrary set of legal rules that judges are given to make the decisions in your lives. That is not how we have been brought up to view them, however. Rather, we have been taught to see them as representing what is just and fair and right. In short, we have been persuaded to see them, not as legal rules, but as legal rights.

When we change legal rules into legal rights, we do a number of things. The first is to sanctify those rules. They are no longer just a set of arbitrary rules designed to solve a problem and answer a question. Rather, they become our God-given entitlements. The second is to credit them as alone being able to provide us with the right answer to that question. Finally, we persuade ourselves that, should we employ any other procedure, we are bound to get it wrong and be left with the wrong answer.

Let us consider this. If you look to legal rules, will they leave you with the right answer to your question and thereby solve your problem? In other words, are you justified in having the same confidence in the application of legal rules that you have in the application of mathematical rules? The answer, of course, is no. Nor will it be difficult to demonstrate this. All that it will take is a little thought experiment. Suppose I were to suggest that instead of employing a mathematician from your own state to do the adding, you employ one from another state? Will you have any problem with this? Of course not. What difference would it make what state the mathematician was from?

But now suppose that I were to suggest that you let a lawyer from another state add up your legal rights. In other words, suppose I suggested that rather than looking to the laws of your own state to get the answer, you look instead to the laws of another state? You are not likely to feel very comfortable doing this, because while mathematicians in every state apply the same rules, you know that lawyers in different states do not. The legal rules that courts apply vary from state to state, and that will bother you. You will not be sure whether the legal rules that are used in another state will help you or hurt you.

That is the first problem with the application of legal rules. They could not possibly leave you with the right answer to your question when, unlike the rules of mathematics, they vary from state to state.

But there is an even more basic problem with legal rules, one that would not be cured even if, like the rules of mathematics, they were the same everywhere. That is the fact that, particularly as they are applied by lawyers in adversarial divorce proceedings, they will not leave you with any answer. Rather, all they will leave you with is just so many conflicting legal opinions.

Before I explain this, let me ask you a question. Would you shop in a supermarket if you knew that upon adding up your purchases, the clerks at each of the checkout counters will give you a different answer (amount) as to what you owe? Needless to say, you wouldn't. In fact, you would probably report the supermarket to the Better Business Bureau. Yet that is exactly what will happen when the two of you go off to the legal supermarket and ask lawyers to do the adding.

Consider this. Why is it that when you ask a mathematical question (How much do my purchases add up to?) you will always be given the same answer but when you ask a legal question (What do my legal rights add up to?) the two of you will invariably be given different answers? There are two reasons. The first is that the numbers that mathematicians employ come with assigned weights. That is why one mathematician does not assign more or less weight to those numbers than another. The second is that all mathematicians follow the same procedure; one does not add and the other subtract. That is why all mathematicians will give you the same answer to your question. It is also why it is not necessary to employ two separate mathematicians. One will do.

The same, unfortunately, is not true when it comes to legal questions. First, unlike numbers, the considerations that the law employs do not come with assigned weights. Rather, they have such weight as a lawyer can persuade a judge to give them. Second, unlike mathematicians, lawyers are not required to apply them in the same way. Rather, it is perfectly permissible for one lawyer to add and for the other to subtract—for example, for one lawyer to say that the age of the parties or the length of their marriage should have a positive effect on (increase) what one party receives, and for the other to say that it should have a negative effect on (decrease) it.

But there is an even more critical problem with the application of legal rules that causes them to leave you with just so many different opinions. Unlike mathematicians, lawyers do not apply the rules of their trade to get an answer. They apply them to make a case for their client, the best possible case that they can. Thus, while a lawyer may say that all that he wants is what is fair to you, what he really wants, and what he has been retained to get, is what is best for you. And what is best for you, at least as a lawyer defines it, is for you to get as much as you can and to give as little as you have to.

Unfortunately, when you combine the indeterminacy of legal rules (the fact that they do not have assigned weights or, therefore, add up to one and only one answer) with the fact that, unlike mathematicians, lawyers do not employ them in an academic exercise to get the right answer (that they are legal advocates, not law professors), you are left with more than different answers. You are left with answers that are so far apart that they literally do not have anything to do with one another.

Let me explain this. Unlike the rules of mathematics, the application of legal rules will not leave you with one and only one answer. This would be true even if the rules were applied by a law professor to get an answer, rather than by a divorce lawyer to make a case. Rather, as every lawyer learns in law school, all that they are capable of leaving you with is a "range of possible answers." To understand this, think of two boxes.

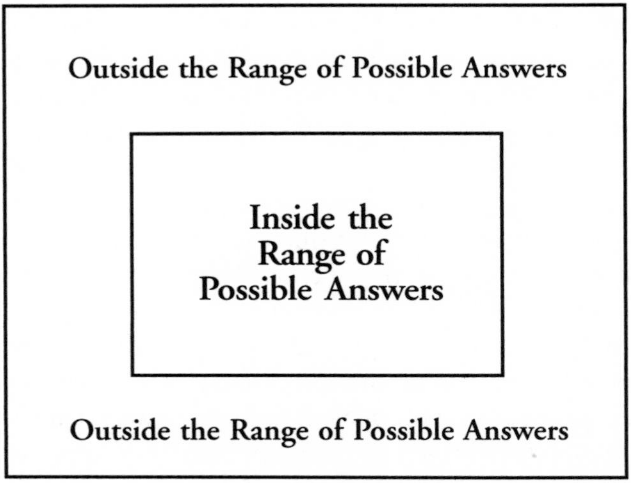

Outside the Range of Possible Answers

Inside the Range of Possible Answers

Outside the Range of Possible Answers

The first, smaller box represents the answers within the range of possible answers. The second, larger box represents those that fall outside the range of possible answers.

As far as a lawyer is concerned, any of the answers within that smaller box are right (legally acceptable). All of the answers outside that smaller box are wrong (legally unacceptable). A lawyer's way to describe those answers is to label those within the smaller box as being "fair" and those outside the smaller box as being "unfair."

But aren't the answers within that smaller box really fair and those outside it really unfair? Of course not. They are only inside or outside the range of possible answers that the application of legal rules will leave you with. All the terms "fair" and "unfair" do is prejudice the issue. All they do is cause you to give more credit to the answers within the range of possible answers than they deserve. It is simply a legal slight-of-hand trick designed to prevent you from seeing what you are not supposed to see, which is that the answers are only inside the box or outside the box. Ironically, many of the answers inside the box could actually be "unfair" just as many of those outside the box could actually be "fair."

This brings me back to what I said earlier, namely that the combination of the law's indeterminacy and the fact that lawyers apply the law to make a case rather than to get an answer will necessarily leave the two of you with answers that literally have nothing to do with one another. There are two reasons for this. The first, as I said, is that the range of answers that you will be left with will be very large, particularly as they are applied by divorce lawyers. The second is that when the two of you consult separate lawyers, neither of you will be given a complete (accurate) picture of that range. Rather, you will each be shown only a limited portion of it. One of you will be shown the answers on the far right side, most favorable to you, and the other the answers on the far left side, most favorable to him or her.

The Range of Possible Answers

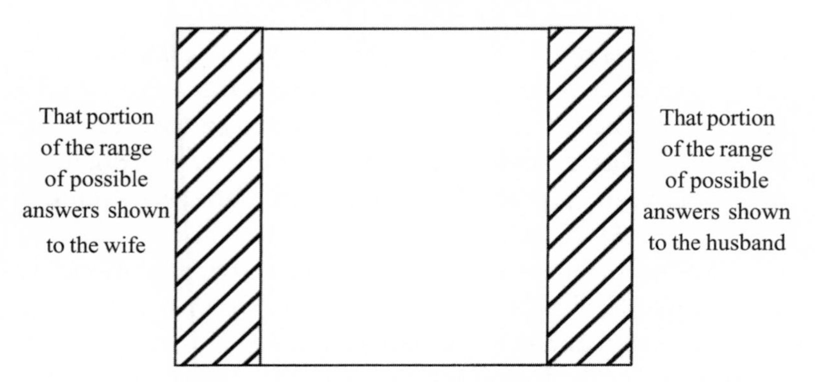

That is why when your husband (or wife) tells you the answer that he was given by his lawyer, you will view it as nothing but an answer given in bad faith. What else could it be when three different lawyers told you just the opposite?

If you were to ask your respective lawyers how they are going to solve this problem, what they will tell you is that they are going to negotiate an agreement. What they will not tell you, however, is that in giving you answers that literally do not have anything to do with one another, they have made a negotiated settlement all but impossible. That is why most cases are concluded not by the negotiating skills of either of the parties' attorneys, but by attrition. The parties get so worn down that they simply give in and give up.

Consider this. Suppose that a husband and wife go off to separate lawyers and the wife is told that she is legally entitled to receive support for eleven years and her husband is told that he has no legal obligation to support her for more than nine years. How will they be able to resolve this? Very easily. They can agree on ten years. It is called a compromise, and we are all brought up to compromise.

But now, suppose that when they go off to their separate lawyers, the wife is told that she is legally entitled to receive support for at least fifteen years and her husband is told that he would be a fool were he to agree to give her support for more than five years. Now they will have a problem. It is no longer possible to resolve the matter by splitting the difference. That is because increasing the size of the range of possible answers does more than add to the problem. It changes the meaning of a settlement. There is no length of time between five years and fifteen years that the two of them can agree on that will not leave one of them, and probably both of them, coming away feeling a fool.

This, unfortunately, is the effect of sanctifying legal rules as representing legal rights. It is also the effect of then employing those rules to make a case for one of you rather than to solve a problem for both of you. Now you can better understand why, if the issue is settled other than by going to court, it will only be by attrition. In the example I gave, the wife's lawyer cannot possibly suggest to her that she accept support for ten years when he has just told her that she is legally entitled to receive it for at least fifteen years. Nor, for the same reason, can the husband's lawyer suggest that to him. Put another way, having shown each of them such narrow and very different portions of the range of possible answers, it will be impossible for both the wife's lawyer and the husband's lawyer to leave them with what they were told they are legally entitled to. That is also why each of the parties will invariably come away feeling that they have suffered a terrible injustice.

What is the answer here? Obviously, if you want the same answer, or at least a far narrower and more accurate picture of the range of possible answers, you will have to go off together and ask the question of one lawyer rather than two.

Unfortunately, that suggestion will cause divorce lawyers to go crazy. Incredibly, they will even argue that it is unethical. In support of this, they will invoke one of our adversarial legal system's most sacred cows. It is called "conflicting interests," and when divorce lawyers look at the two of you, that is all that they see. This, supposedly, is what makes it inappropriate for you to use the law constructively—for the two of you to go off together and get an answer to your question and thereby solve your problem. It is also what condemns you to have to use the law destructively, as a weapon—to go off and do legal battle with one another.

When all is said and done, what does it mean to say that the two of you have conflicting interests? It just means that you would each like to hear different answers to the same question. One of you would like to hear fifteen years and the other five years. But it doesn't change the answer. Nor does it make any more sense to engage in a game of legal chess to get that answer than it would to employ a coin.

A lawyer's insistence that your conflicting interests render it inappropriate for the two of you to consult with one lawyer to get an answer to your question is just a smoke screen. It is simply an abstraction designed to prevent you from seeing what you are not supposed to see, namely, that our legal system has been organized as a contest—as a game of legal chess. But there is no law that says that legal rules have to be applied in that manner. Nor does it make any sense to do that.

Ironically, if the two of you had a difference of opinion with respect to anything else, you would understand this. Suppose, for example, that the two of you could not agree on whether your child should undergo a particular medical treatment. Suppose someone were to insist that, because you had conflicting opinions here, the two of you had to go off and consult with separate physicians. Would that make any sense to you? Obviously not. In fact, you would dismiss it as nonsense. It is no less nonsense because the opinion you are seeking is a legal one rather than a medical one. Without question, the two of you might decide to get a second opinion, but again, you would go off and get it together.

There is one last thing that you must keep in mind when it comes to the application of legal rules, and that is that a legal answer is not there for the asking. Rather, it is the endpoint of a process. Thus, if you want the answer that you will get by applying legal rules, you will have to employ the procedure that the law provides for that purpose. Moreover, you will have to see it to the end since there is no other way to get it. Unfortunately, that procedure is an adversarial one. What that means is that if you want the answer that the law provides, the two of you will have to become adversaries and go off to court to get it.

CHAPTER 33

SETTLING FOR LESS THAN YOU ARE LEGALLY ENTITLED TO

All too often the least able lawyer in the courtroom is the one who will decide the case.

Why do husbands and wives retain lawyers? Because they believe that lawyers will vouchsafe their legal rights—see to it that they get everything that they are entitled to under the law. How will they do that? By employing the rules and procedures that the law provides.

This raises a question. Why do lawyers so rarely go to court and employ the rules and procedures they tout so much? Why, as they admit (actually boast), do they settle more than ninety percent of their cases rather than allow those legal rules and procedures to play themselves out? A mathematician employed to solve a mathematical problem would never abort the application of the rules and procedures he employs and "settle" the problem (whatever that means). Rather, he will always see it to the end. He does not want just any answer. He wants the right answer, which is why he employs mathematical rules and procedures in the first place.

This is another little secret about adversarial divorce proceedings no one has told you. Again, it is something that you do not see because you are not supposed to see. That secret is that divorcing husbands and wives invariably come away with less than they were told they were legally entitled to.

Why does this happen? The first reason may surprise you. Though lawyers forever talk about your "legal rights," the truth is that they do not have as much faith in the legal rules courts apply as they would lead you to believe. That is why, unlike mathematicians, rather than allow those rules to play themselves out as they will, lawyers are forever trying to manipulate them. It is for the same reason that they try as hard as they do to slant the playing field to their advantage. Having very little confidence in how legal rules will play out, they do not trust them. That is also why they settle so many of their cases. They are afraid to go to court. They know that the legal rules they laud so much are just as likely to hurt you as they are to help you.

The second reason lawyers settle so many of their cases rather than go to court may surprise you as well. It is that they have even less faith in the judges who will apply those rules. Judges, after all, are not moral philosophers. They are very ordinary men and women. Thus, if they express opinions as to what is fair and just and equitable, it is not because they are more qualified to make those judgments than the rest of us. It is because they have been given the power to do so. Am I being disrespectful to our judicial legal system? I don't think so. I am just telling the truth.

A number of years ago, when I had just begun to do the work I now do, I ran into a judge I knew quite well at the bar association. Like myself, he had been an established divorce lawyer before he went on the bench. He had apparently heard of what I was doing and expressed an interest in it. When I asked him if he would like to sit in and observe a mediation, he said he would, and we arranged for him to do that. Purposely, I wanted to have him sit in with a couple with whom I was meeting for the first time, as his presence would seem more natural.

On the night in question, at his request, I introduced him to the couple as being simply a divorce lawyer who was interested in mediation. Rather than participate in our discussions, he sat to my left, slightly behind me.

Since this was just a "get-to-know-you meeting," I initially did most of the talking. As the meeting proceeded, I became less and less conscious of the fact that there was someone else in the room besides the couple and me. At some point, our discussions turned to adversarial divorce proceedings and what would happen if they went to court. In response to something one of them said, and completely oblivious to the fact that there was anyone else in the room, I said, "I mean no disrespect, but there is no important decision affecting my life that I would ever let a judge make if I could avoid it." At that point, I remembered there was a judge actually sitting in the room with us, and, somewhat embarrassingly, I glanced over my shoulder at him. When I did, I saw that he was silently nodding in agreement.

Most divorce lawyers I knew felt themselves fortunate when their cases were assigned to this judge. It was not just because he was a good jurist. It was that his intelligence was balanced by his humility. He knew the inevitable fallibility of all our judgments, particularly those that we make in other people's lives. That is why he felt it was better that they make those decisions themselves rather than leave them to him.

Unfortunately, this judge was the exception rather than the rule. Most are nowhere near as able. That is not the problem. The problem is that, far too often, there is an invariable relationship between a judge's lack of ability and his or her lack of humility. The less able he is, the less humble he will be. As it is said, "Often in error, but never in doubt." Appearing before judges such as this is worse than tossing a coin. It is a crapshoot. Anything can happen. That too, is one of the little secrets about adversarial divorce proceedings. All too often the least able lawyer in the courtroom is the one who will decide the case.

That is also why divorce lawyers settle so many of their cases—settle for less than they told their clients they were legally entitled to. They have no more faith in the judges who will decide their cases than they do in the legal rules that they will use in making their decision.

CHAPTER 34

WHAT TO DO—WHAT NOT TO DO

Doing nothing is also doing something.

As you approach the end of this book, I appreciate that you might be tempted to say to yourself, "Yes, he told me what not to do. But he didn't tell me what to do."

If you read carefully, however, I did. I told you to do nothing. Or, to be more accurate, I told you that all of the things that you will be tempted to do, and that your Greek Chorus of well-wishers will counsel you to do, are the wrong things. I told you that, like the proverbial chicken with its head cut off, following all of that advice will only send you off in a hundred different directions, going nowhere. I told you to resist the temptation to do something just so you won't feel that you aren't doing anything. I told you that going off on your own and resorting to self-help is always how things get out of hand. I told you to stop, think, and take control of what is happening in your life rather than letting it take control of you. Finally, I told you to be realistic in terms of what you have a right to expect and not expect because you live in the real world, not in a lawyer's world of fantasy.

Obviously, there are things that you must do. Principal amongst those is to recognize that, in most instances, the two of you are not going to be able to do this on your own and that you will need help. Not the help of those who will send you off to do battle with one another. Rather, the sound judgment and steady hand of someone who can sit the two of you down, point out all the issues that you must address and resolve, and then help you do that. Contrary to what everyone else will tell you, that is all you should do or need to do.

Think about it. If you are told to do something—for example get yourself a good lawyer—you are being told to go off on your own and to resort to self-help. What will your husband or wife now do? They will do the same thing—go off on their own and get themselves a good lawyer as well. Where does that leave the two of you? It leaves you going off in different directions. It leaves you preparing for your worst nightmare. It leaves you going down the wrong road. That is what I meant when I said at the very outset that if I am going to help you as I would like, I must first point you in the right direction.

What is the right direction? To go off together. If you go off together, neither of you will have to do anything on your own. Nor will you feel the need to. If the rule is business as usual—and that is the only rule that makes sense—there will be nothing that you have to do or feel compelled to do.

I appreciate that this may not seem like doing very much—and you very much want to do something. Ironically, it will take all your effort and all your smarts just to do that. That is because there will be so many fears that will tend to overwhelm you, because there will be so many difficult feelings that will begin to take control of you, and because there will be so many signposts along the way that will point you in the wrong direction.

Let me give you an example. You are trying as hard as you can to keep yourself pointed in the right direction and not be distracted by all of your concerns and all of your fears. But you come to a fork in the road where one of the signs reads: "Yes, I understand. You have been told that you and your husband or wife should go down the road where the two of you will sit down together and address the problems that you now find yourselves faced with. But let me ask you a question. Do you really want to do this on your own? Wouldn't you like to have someone in your corner?"

Like so much of what you will be told, that sounds innocent enough. After all, who wouldn't like to have someone in his or her corner? Be careful. It is not quite as innocent as it appears. Why is that? First, because it is addressed to your fears rather than to your better judgment. Second, because it is has been phrased in a way to get by your rational censor. It sounds better than it reads. To put it another way, it only sounds good so long as you do not think about it. The minute you think about it, it doesn't sound good at all.

What do I mean when I say that it is getting by your rational censor? I mean that it is preventing you from thinking about what you have been told and seeing its necessary implications. What are those implications? If you have someone in your corner, then it is natural to assume that your husband or wife will want to have someone in his or her corner as well. After all, the same logic that appeals to you will appeal to him or her. Even if it didn't initially, it certainly will when they see you come into the discussions with your coach—someone in your corner.

Where does that leave the two of you? Well, if you activate your rational censor and start thinking about what you have been told, things will begin to look a little different. It will start to look as if the two of you are getting ready to go into the ring together to do battle with one another. Why else would each of you need a coach in your corner?

That is why it is going to take so much effort on your part just to keep yourself headed in the right direction. There will be so many things that will distract you and tend to get your eye off the mark. That is why, if you want to do something, content yourself with keeping your eye on the mark. Content yourself by asking where you want to end up and what you will have to do to get there. If you do nothing but that, you will be doing all that you have to do to keep things from getting out of hand. Anyone who has your best interests at heart would not want that to happen. Remember, it is not very difficult to let the genie out of the bottle. It is almost impossible, however, to get him back in.

CHAPTER 35

CONCLUSION

How can it be the end when it is just the beginning?

You have now come to what would normally be considered the end of this book.

But it is not the end. It is just the beginning.

You and your husband or wife will now have to sit down and address many things—with whom your children will live and where, and what time they will spend with each of you; how you will divide your property; what payments, if any, will be made by one of you to the other for his or her support, and for how long; what payments will be made for the support of your children; and many more.

As you go down the road before you, it is inevitable that you will come across rough spots along the way. There may even be times when you will not know in which direction to turn. When that happens, you may stumble and lose your footing. You may even find yourself lost in the dark.

It is then that you will need help. Undoubtedly, there will be all of those voices in the wilderness calling to you and all of those beacons of light on the horizon beckoning to you. You must be careful, however. Do not allow yourself to be seduced by every siren call you hear or by every flickering light you see. If you do, you will certainly go off in the wrong direction and lose your way. Look for the calm and balanced voice. Look for the clear light. Look for the voice that tells you the truth and calls to your better understanding. Look to the light that sends out a steady beam. If you need help, those are the ones that you should follow.

It is obviously not for me to tell you which of those voices or which of those lights you should attend to, the one expressed and cast by this book or the many others that you will encounter along the way. For better or worse, that is a decision that you will have to make for yourself. All that I can say is that the counsel that I have given you is the same counsel that I have given to literally thousands of couples who have come to me over the years who were faced with the same problems that you now find yourself confronted with. I know that it helped them. They have told me so, and thanked me for it.

I can only hope that it will help you. That is why I wrote this book. May you return to it when you need help. May it serve as a constant companion to you along the way.